ON THE
BRINK

ON THE
BRINK

GRACE FOR
THE BURNED-OUT
PASTOR

CLAY WERNER

P U B L I S H I N G

P.O. BOX 817 • PHILLIPSBURG • NEW JERSEY 08865-0817

ISBN: 978-1-59638-898-7 (pbk.)
ISBN: 978-1-59638-899-4 (ePub)
ISBN: 978-1-59638-900-7 (Mobi)

Printed in the United States of America

Library of Congress Cataloging-in-Publication Data

Werner, Clay, 1981-
 On the brink : grace for the burned-out pastor / Clay Werner.
    pages cm
 Includes bibliographical references.
 ISBN 978-1-59638-898-7 (pbk.)
 1. Pastoral theology. I. Title.
 BV4014.W47 2014
 248.8'92--dc23
                                        2014008026

To my bride:
When I've prayed for God to strengthen me,
he often answers through your heart and hands.
"Many women have done excellently, but you surpass them all"
(Prov. 31:29).

To my group of men in the mountains:
Through our few years together already,
your words and counsel have meant more than you'll ever know.
"The tongue of the wise brings healing" (Prov. 12:18).

CONTENTS

FOREWORD

THIS IS A RARE and much-needed book.

It is much needed because pastors experience loneliness and discouragement, even depression and despair, more often than most church members (and even other pastors) realize. Hard statistics show an alarming pattern of pastoral attrition in the early years of ministry. If you are a pastor, you may not be on the brink of letting go and dropping out this week, but you may remember your own counterpart to Clay Werner's days of soul anguish in the solitude of the Smoky Mountains. And quite likely you have a colleague in ministry, perhaps in a nearby congregation, who is even now where Clay was then. If you are a Christian who has a pastor (I hope you do—we all need shepherding through men called by Jesus, the Chief Shepherd), then Pastor Werner's testimony and his gospel-grounded counsel will enlighten your empathy and inform your prayers for your pastor.

This is a rare book because of its extraordinary blend of ruthless transparency, mature wisdom, conscience-probing questions, biblical and theological insight, and—most importantly—its profound grasp of how the grace of God in the gospel of Christ meets pastors in the depths of discouragement. If I didn't know Clay Werner, I would doubt that a book with such maturity and wisdom could be written after less than a decade in pastoral ministry. If I didn't know Clay, I would be surprised to hear a pastor (of any age) so thoroughly shed his veneer of competence and confidence, inviting readers (including many still hiding behind their own façades in quiet desperation) into the wrenching struggles of his heart. If I didn't know Clay, I might expect a book on dealing with depression in the pastorate to lead me to the counselor's couch—which, admittedly, sometimes helps. Instead, we have a book that leads us to Christ's cross, which, when we discover its implications, never fails to humble as it heals and heartens, giving solid hope for strong perseverance.

I love Clay and his wife, Liz, as a brother and sister in Christ too much to have wished for him the ministerial traumas that he has undergone or to have wished for them the sufferings (both ministry and family related) that they have experienced together. But I am grateful that God's sovereign agenda for them is infinitely wiser and more loving than my limited perspective. Through the crucible Clay has been refined and formed into a more serviceable servant of Christ and witness to the Savior's grace. His fellow pastors and elders have recognized the Lord's work in "maturing" Clay beyond his years by choosing him to lead a committee charged to care for pastors' hearts and well-being. As he bears witness and brings counsel, his words ring true. He speaks with blunt realism and tender empathy as one who vividly recalls the darkness. For that very reason, he speaks with bold indictment of the idols of the heart that tempt pastors and lead them into darkness. He also speaks with bold confidence in the grace of Jesus, who leads his hurting servants out of darkness into the light of his mercy and his presence.

Be forewarned: in chapters 1 through 5, the diagnosis of the sources of discouragement and despair in pastoral ministry may cause severe discomfort. In the midst of soul-stirring biblical exposition and insights into the practicality of sound theology, our author relentlessly confronts us with the daily stresses that elicit from pastors all sorts of faithless, prideful, self-pitying, and self-defeating reactions. But just when you begin to wonder whether *On the Brink* has anything to offer beyond "Misery loves company," guilt trips, and "stiff upper lip" stoicism, Clay turns your attention to the Son of God, who loved you and died for you; to the freedom of grounding your identity in his grace, rather than in your ministerial productivity; and to the enduring hope that Jesus offers by letting us in on the secret that he tends his farm and expands his kingdom in gradual, unimpressive, but invincible ways.

Dennis E. Johnson, Ph.D.
Professor of Practical Theology,
Westminster Seminary California
Associate Pastor, New Life Presbyterian Church,
Escondido, California

ACKNOWLEDGMENTS

NEW TESTAMENT scholar William L. Lane once remarked, "When God gives a gift, he wraps it in a person."[1] The greatest earthly gift I have is my wife, Liz. Through our years together, she has been a living and breathing "sermon in shoes," as my friend Joe Novenson often says, of God's steadfast love that never cools down and never gives up. Thanks, Liz, for your enduring faithfulness, beautiful smile, and simple joy through these years. I also want to thank each of my five children—Isaac, Claire, David, Noah, and Andrew—for their faithfulness in always welcoming Daddy home with huge smiles and hugs.

Early in my seminary career, I had a professor who not only was willing to say hard things to make me think more deeply and live more humbly, but also became a pastor to me. Dr. Dennis Johnson and his wife, Jane, brought gracious words and a healing touch as they invited Liz and me into their hearts and lives. To say that he has had a big impact on my life would be an enormous understatement. I want to thank him for his love and counsel through the years, his ability to help me and many others see the glory of Christ in the Word, and the tremendous amount of work he did in helping me along the way with this project.

I also want to thank Pastor Joe Novenson. He has been an incredible mentor through the years, holding my hand and filling my heart when life seemed to be unraveling. In the midst of his busy schedule, he has always taken time to comfort, challenge, and encourage a young pastor who often has no clue what he is doing. Joe and his wife, Barb, through letters, phone calls, and meals together, have helped Liz and me endure by helping our hearts focus more on the treasures of grace we have in Christ.

1. Quoted in Michael Card, *The Walk: The Life-Changing Journey of Two Friends* (Grand Rapids: Discovery House Publishers, 2006), 4.

As you read along, you will notice the role an elder played in recovering my heart from a very dark time. He has always brought profound encouragement through his wise counsel and faithful guidance through the Scriptures. Many of the things I write about in this book are things I've learned by listening to and watching him.

Thanks also to the leadership and staff of P&R Publishing. In particular, Amanda Martin and Julia Craig have provided enormous help along the way with the manuscript. I am also grateful for their willingness to allow me to seek to comfort others with the same amazing and sustaining grace that has comforted me on this journey (2 Cor. 1:3–5).

"When I am wounded he heals me; when I faint, he revives me again. . . . Grace reigns. Be that my motto." —John Newton[2]

2. *Wise Counsel: John Newton's Letters to John Ryland Jr.*, ed. Grant Gordon (Carlisle, PA: Banner of Truth Trust, 2009), 170.

INTRODUCTION

"Consider him who endured from sinners such hostility against himself, so that you may not grow weary or fainthearted."
—Hebrews 12:3

"Never, never, never believe any war will be smooth and easy, or that anyone who embarks on the strange voyage can measure the tides and hurricanes he will encounter."
—Winston Churchill[1]

ONE LOOK AT JESUS hanging on the cross will teach you that if you make a conscious decision to deeply and sacrificially love sinners, it's going to hurt something awful. I mean really, really, really bad. When the tears from the pain and agony and frustration and exhaustion of ministry cover the eyes of your heart, you begin to lose sight of the incredible power and amazing hope that the gospel of Jesus Christ gives to you.

One look at Jesus will also teach you that if God loved us even to the point of death on a cross, he'll provide strength to endure and hope to persevere through the incredible and humanly impossible calling of loving *fellow* sinners. I'm still slowly learning these truths, and I would bet that if you've picked up this book and are reading this page, you may be, as I've been a thousand times in my first five years of ministry, on the verge of throwing in the towel.

Paul's words to Timothy have rung in my head often: "I urge you to stay." Paul's term *urge* was also used in battle by commanders to force their

---

1. Quoted in Victor Davis Hanson, *The Father of Us All: War and History, Ancient and Modern* (New York: Bloomsbury Press, 2010), 187.

men back to the front of battle when they were running in retreat. This reminds me of a scene from *The Red Badge of Courage*:

> He, too, threw down his gun and fled. He ran like a rabbit. . . . He yelled with fright and swung about. For a moment, in the great clamor, he was like a proverbial chicken. . . . He lost the direction of safety. Destruction threatened him from all points. . . . Directly he began to speed toward the rear in great leaps. . . . On his face was all the horror of those things which he imagined.[2]

There was a point in my own ministry when I too wanted to run. In one position as an assistant pastor and in another as a senior pastor, I had seen, heard, and experienced enough that made me consider any other job as a viable option in order to keep my sanity, and even my faith, intact. Like the young man in *The Red Badge of Courage*, I looked forward to victory and success, but thought about tucking tail and running away the moment the big guns started firing at me.

Four years earlier, I had entered into gospel ministry eager, excited, and theologically trained, thinking that three years of seminary and an internship had prepared me. But I was, in reality, extremely naive. Early on I had listened to an address that the president of my denomination's seminary gave, which revealed that many pastors leave the ministry for good after only five years.[3] My initial thoughts were, "C'mon! Have a backbone. Nobody said ministry was going to be a cakewalk. I can't believe these guys are only lasting five years. Good riddance if they can't endure that long. The church needs pastors who are real men and who are tough and can last." You probably cringe just reading that. Now I do too.

After only four years of ministry, I was ready to throw in the towel, feeling more than comfortable to be a statistic. Heart-crushing and soul-clogging memories began to fill my mind. When I was young, the church I grew up in split because the pastor had an affair with someone in the church. He merely took his followers five miles down the road to start another church. When I was in high school, hardly ever attending church

2. Stephen Crane, *The Red Badge of Courage* (Huntington, WV: Empire Books, 2012), 39.

3. Studies by The Fuller Institute and George Barna show that over 1,700 pastors leave the ministry every month, while 1,300 are terminated by their churches, often without cause. For these alarming statistics and more, see "Statistics in the Ministry," *Pastoral Care Inc.*, accessed September 9, 2013, http://www.pastoralcareinc.com/statistics.

at all, another pastor was let go over morality issues. I hated the church and wanted nothing to do with it, ever. Ironically, God saved me through some faithful friends who shared the gospel with me right before I got to college, and I immediately became involved with a faithful gospel-preaching church. It was there that I began to sense a call to ministry due to the faithful preaching of, and brief interaction with, the senior pastor. As soon as I entered seminary, he took his own life. Once again, I was crushed.

The past horror stories and the battles that were currently going on made me greatly doubt the life-giving, heart-transforming power of the gospel of Jesus Christ. I was on a spiritual drip, barely alive. I even wondered if the resurrection was true. But one thing I knew for sure: I was done with gospel ministry.

Then God showed up. Not in any miraculous vision. I didn't hear any strange voice or get a message from an angel sent from God. I read and reread Exodus and Numbers, all four gospels, Paul's life, N. T. Wright's *The Resurrection of the Son of God*, and a book from an old favorite of mine, Jonathan Edwards, *Charity and Its Fruits*. Slowly God breathed life back into me. Slowly my idealistic vision of ministry was being crushed, and the reality of the gospel began once again to enliven my soul.

I'm sure you have your own stories of being bruised and beaten up and other stories of letdowns, shakedowns, bitter fights, draining meetings, and the list could go on forever. My hope is that you'll take a journey with me and relearn some of the basic truths of the gospel and hammer out implications along the way that sometimes we totally miss.

Before we begin our journey together, I want to look briefly at two things that will be essential to keep in the back of your mind as you read. The first is understanding the difference between a theology of glory and a theology of the cross, and the second is Kevin Vanhoozer's concept of "fitting participation" in the drama of redemption.

To begin with, although many pastors profess a theology of the cross, they often function unconsciously with a theology of glory. A theology of glory maintains that we come from glory and are headed for glory, and in between we strive to stay on "the glory road."[4] Like the young soldier, these

---

4. For a brief explanation of these two theologies, see especially Gerhard O. Forde, *On Being a Theologian of the Cross: Reflections on Luther's Heidelberg Disputation, 1518* (Grand Rapids: Eerdmans, 1997), 1–22.

leaders expect little suffering and many successes, and either run in fear or remain with bitterness and anger when things break down. Hardship, suffering, self-denial, and patience are all anathema to a heart driven by a theology of glory. A theology of the cross, however, accepts suffering as the lot of any Christian, realizing that just as Christ suffered and then entered into glory, so we must follow the same path.

Second, Kevin Vanhoozer writes that proper doctrine enables us to understand how to have "fitting participation" in the continuing drama of redemption.[5] When we have an underlying theology of glory of which we are often completely unaware, fitting participation in the drama of redemption as leader-servants of God's people will always remain an impossibility. The first part of this book, chapters 1–5, deals with these realities. Chapter 1 will lay the foundation as we look at the life of Moses through the lens of *simul iustus et peccator* (at the same time just and sinner). Chapter 2 will explore the external difficulties of ministry, while chapter 3 will dive into the inward idolatries that reside in the hearts of many ministry leaders. Chapter 4 will take a look at how we often possess an accurate theology that is not being lived with a heart-level functionality. The first part concludes with chapter 5 outlining the variety of reasons for potentially leaving ministry for another calling.

The second part uses the theology of the cross to explore how the gospel guides, equips, and empowers leaders to endure through the incredible joys and the dreadful pains of ministry. In other words, the gospel will reveal how to "fittingly participate" as a servant of Christ's bride. Chapter 6 will outline how the resurrection restores our hearts and our hope, so that we can enter back into ministry. Chapter 7 shows that we need to be motivated by love, while chapter 8 considers how Jesus' rescue of chief sinners inspires leaders to jump into every aspect of ministry. Chapter 9 will look at servanthood, and then chapter 10 will explore how to serve in the midst of significant conflict. Chapter 11 will round off the study by standing in awe of God's steadfast love.

I've sought throughout to maintain a "reporting from the battle" feel. I've read other books by older and more experienced men that convey that they've gone through the battles of ministry and are reflecting on what

---

5. See Kevin Vanhoozer, *The Drama of Doctrine: A Canonical-Linguistic Approach to Christian Theology* (Louisville: Westminster John Knox, 2005), esp. 77–114.

they've learned.[6] This book has much more of a feel that the battle is still very current and that the temptation to quit is still very real as I myself am still only in my seventh year of ministry—which is why I need counselors and "conversation partners" throughout, like John Calvin, John Newton, Francis Schaeffer, Martin Lloyd-Jones, and other veterans from whom rookies can learn. I am also the current chair of a regional committee that oversees the spiritual welfare of pastors in over fifty churches, which has allowed me to see both the incredible blessings and the profound burdens that many other pastors have to walk through on a daily basis.

The young soldier in *The Red Badge of Courage* lost the direction of safety in the battle as he ran from the chaos. Strangely and paradoxically, in ministry the "direction of safety" is toward the chaos and difficulty, because that is precisely where God promises to meet with and strengthen us. Are you ready to run toward the battle?

6. Charles Bridges, *The Christian Ministry* (Carlisle, PA: Banner of Truth Trust, 2001); Charles Spurgeon, *Lectures to My Students* (Pasadena: Pilgrim Publications, 1990). More recent treatments that I highly recommend are Zack Eswine, *Sensing Jesus: Life and Ministry as a Human Being* (Wheaton: Crossway, 2013); Paul David Tripp, *Dangerous Calling: Confronting the Unique Challenges of Pastoral Ministry* (Wheaton: Crossway, 2012); Dave Kraft, *Leaders Who Last* (Wheaton: Crossway, 2010); Michael A. Milton, *Hit by Friendly Fire: What to Do When Christians Hurt You* (Eugene, OR: Wipf and Stock, 2008).

1

SEEING HIM WHO IS INVISIBLE

AFTER A REMARKABLY grueling and severely discouraging leadership meeting in the middle of a churchwide, long-term, multiyear conflict, I met with an elder while I sobbed uncontrollably. I was tired and exhausted, had lost all hope, questioned why I ever went into ministry, and practically promised that he would have my resignation in the mail in a few days. In my heart, I had really committed to quitting, demitting the ministry, and moving closer to family to get a high school teaching job, coach football, and be a rafting guide during the summers (this was my original life goal before God seemingly messed it up by calling me into ministry). In the meantime, I was going to go sit next to a river in the middle of the Smoky Mountains and have a temper tantrum with God.

It was in those mountains that I picked up my Bible and prayed about what I needed to read to find encouragement. I read and reread and cried through Exodus and Numbers. I marked all the times Israel rebelled. Angrily, I circled every time the word *grumble* or *complain* showed up. Pridefully, I paid careful attention to how difficult it must have been for Moses to lead a people who were so hard-hearted and rebellious, immature and impossible. I began to sympathize with Moses. If he and I could have met at Starbucks, he would have gone beyond sympathy and actually *empathized* with me and all I was going through. I was sure he could give me some wise counsel. Perhaps he would tell me to get out while I could, while I still had a little skin left, and do something less painful and debilitating than leading God's people. I felt like Moses' anger justified my own anger.

Next I turned to the Gospels and marked every time the disciples failed or said something silly or disappointed Jesus. I paid careful attention to the times when Jesus was deeply grieved in his heart over the hardness of his own disciples. Deep down in a hidden place in my heart, I secretly whispered to myself, "See! Even Jesus can sympathize with how difficult leadership is. If he sat with me at Starbucks, we could swap stories about how awful and tiring leading sheep can be!" At this point, I was becoming pretty happy with myself—perhaps I could continue in ministry. Just follow the example of Moses and Jesus; commit to getting thicker skin and a deeper resolve; commit to being more vocal and rebuking people more often. I was on the fence, not knowing which way to go: was Jesus leading me to resign or not to resign? I was hoping for a still small voice, but all I heard was rippling water and the sound of tourists driving by.

But there was one thing I was missing, and it was the most important thing—the gospel. I had totally missed it. I had a blame-retardant coating on my heart and refused to see the sin inside, yet I was relentless in pointing out the flaws of others. I identified myself as a leader, pastor, and shepherd, and had forgotten that I too was a hard-hearted, rebellious, idolatrous, angry, frustrated, slow-to-learn, impatient, prayerless sheep-disciple filled with self-righteous anger, fair-weather faith, and unrealistic and dangerous expectations of the sheep in the congregation I pastored. I wasn't Moses or Jesus, but one of the complaining Israelites and one of the faltering disciples. The story of their faltering and their failure was the story of my heart. I was like Israel, constantly wanting to quit when things got tough, feeling entitled to better living conditions and more faithful followers. I was like the disciples, constantly grieving Jesus with my hard heart and slowness to learn.

I wept for hours. I had superficially prayed through phrases from Psalm 19 and 139: "show me my hidden faults"; "know my heart and thoughts and show me if there is any grievous way in me." I just never really expected God to answer. But he did—again and again and again. My hard heart began to be softened through a gospel-focused, Spirit-empowered repentance. I wasn't called to "be like Moses" and go back and tough it out. No, I was called to go back and keep the eyes of my heart firmly placed on the author and perfecter of my faith—the always perfect, never grumbling, always interceding, forgiving, patient, compassionate leader of the new and better exodus—Jesus Christ.

He wasn't just confronted with the grumbling and hard-heartedness of myself and all his people, but bore its condemnation and never complained—not once.

He responded with complete perfection to his Father's will and never complained about it, but humbly submitted to becoming a curse for me and all the other grumbling and almost-quitting leaders of his people. He who never grumbled was condemned as a grumbler so that I might be accepted by the Father.

I took along a commentary that one of my seminary professors had written, and the knife of repentance was thrust deeper into my soul. In a powerful passage, he states that much of our frustrations come from trying to be the "functional saviors" of our people. If we could just "fix" our people, he writes, we would have a sense of personal achievement and joy.

"We would then be able to bask in the glory of our renovation, feeding our pride and sense of self-worth. The Holy Spirit, however, is not eager to share his glory. He bears his fruit in the lives of his people in *his* season, not ours, so that it may be clearly seen that the work is entirely of him."[1]

I was trying to be a savior and play the role of the Spirit as a leader in the church, and I finally began to let go of the reigns of the universe and put the situation and the results back into the hands of my loving Father. By the faithful work of the Spirit, my eyes were redirected to the splendor and wonder of the gospel once again, and I sought for the remainder of my time to submit myself to the gospel surgery that Jesus had already begun in my life. I sought to place my own gospel renovation and the gospel renovation of the church I pastored back into the lap of the Holy Spirit, trusting in his sovereign work and sovereign timing—in my heart first, and then in theirs.

I'm always encouraged when I see leaders in the Bible want to give up. They deal with the same external problems and internal heart struggles that we do. It is here that Moses is a particularly helpful example. With our hearts focused on the gospel, we are now ready to dive into his story, which may have many similarities to your story. As we do, I'll use Jonathan Edwards's chapter on long-suffering in his book *Charity and Its Fruits* as a lens through which to read the story of Moses and gain pastoral insight for our own day-to-day ministry. If anyone had the pastorally earned authority

1. Iain Duguid, *Numbers: God's Presence in the Wilderness* (Wheaton: Crossway, 2006), 254.

to write on such a subject it was Edwards, who himself had gone through his fair share of crushing conflict.[2]

WHAT MOSES ENDURED

"Overwhelmingly difficult" doesn't even begin to describe the life and calling of Moses. Perhaps "outrageously difficult" gets closer. His experience was heart crushing, soul depleting, mind numbing, strength sapping, frustrating, and exhausting. Reading the story of Moses in Exodus and Numbers in one sitting almost makes you wonder whether Moses was a real person. How can any mere human survive or even put up with being "provoked" for forty years (Heb. 3:15–17) by a hard-hearted, forgetful, stubborn, and rebellious people that he himself has helped to deliver? If I'm provoked for four minutes, I begin to lose it—but forty years? Can this really be true?

Edwards begins his chapter on long-suffering by stating the obvious but frequently forgotten truth that the ways in which we will be hurt or disappointed by others are various and innumerable.[3] This is something that anyone involved in ministry is painfully reminded of on an almost daily basis. Before we move forward, then, it will be crucial to understand *what* Moses endured before we seek to answer the question of *how* he endured.

His life began with difficulty. His mother had to hide him and then send him away lest he be killed. He was raised by someone other than his own parents and in a foreign land. After seeing the suffering of his people, he initially tried to deliver them, but they didn't understand him (Acts 7:23–28). He spent the next forty years in the howling wilderness. Would you have given up yet?

He then faced increasingly more difficult situations, with increasingly more challenging people. Early on in his calling, after a remarkable display of God's terrifying, potentially death-causing glory, God told Moses that he would deliver the Israelites from the hand of Pharaoh. But think about it: God basically told him, "Moses, I want you to deliver my people. I'm going to crush Pharaoh into the dust of the earth. But just know this: when you

2. To see the reasons behind some of Edwards's ministerial difficulties, which led to his eventual expulsion from the church he pastored, see Iain H. Murray, *Jonathan Edwards: A New Biography* (Carlisle, PA: Banner of Truth Trust, 2000), 271–87.

3. Jonathan Edwards, *Charity and Its Fruits* (Carlisle, PA: Banner of Truth Trust, 2000), 67–71.

tell him what you're supposed to tell him, I'm going to harden his heart so that he won't listen to you!" Interesting plan. Would you have given up yet?

God told Moses that the Israelites would listen to his voice (Ex. 3:18). Yet later on, we read, "they did not listen to Moses" (Ex. 6:9), and Moses complains to God about this very thing (6:12). In fact, you could accurately say that the exodus and the forty years in the wilderness were character-ized by the Israelites refusing to listen to Moses (Acts 7:39). Have you ever wondered whether Moses began to think that God might have lied to him? What was God doing? Could his word be trusted? In the early days of Moses' calling, God hardened Pharaoh's heart, the people would not listen, and his life was threatened. Would you have given up yet?

Let's get a more detailed picture of what Moses endured. *Hatred* would be an accurate term for how his own people frequently thought about him (Ex. 2:15; 5:21). If Moses didn't provide *what* the people wanted, *when* they wanted it, stoning him always remained a possible option (Ex. 17:4; Num. 14:10). Although Moses was "very meek, more than all people who were on the face of the earth" (Num. 12:3), the people described Moses as a supremely prideful man, seeking his own glory in their deaths (Num. 16:3, 12–14). Israel could also be described as having spiritual Alzheimer's or redemption amnesia and never being cured. They forgot God's deliv-ering power in the plagues when they were chased by Pharaoh's army (Ex. 14:10–14). They forgot the parting of the Red Sea when they were confronted with the report of the spies returning from the Promised Land (Num. 13:31). They forgot the majesty of God's glory and the impor-tance of his authority and "turned aside quickly" to other idols (Ex. 32:8; Num. 25:1–3). They forgot God's severe judgment on grumblers and rebels *the day before*, and continued grumbling the next day (Num. 16:41). After seeing displays of God's glory in the pillar of fire and the cloud, hearing his voice from Mt. Sinai and his commands from Moses, enjoying his provi-sion of water and manna and quail—after forty years of God's incredible faithfulness—Israel had learned nothing and remained hard-hearted and rebellious. Would you have given up yet?

We should not forget two more things that Moses repeatedly endured: grumbling and betrayal. The Israelites had a selective and faulty memory, thinking that Egypt was paradise—where the weather was always nice, the food was always great, and life was always good—and supposing that anything less than going back was idiotic (Ex. 16:2, 7–9, 12; Num. 11:4–6; 14:1–4; 20:2–5; 21:5). They grumbled because God's provision wasn't as lavish and tasty as they would have liked (Ex. 15:24; 17:2). They grumbled because they were envious of Moses. In fact, to put it bluntly, in their minds anything and everything was a justifiable reason for grumbling (see especially Num. 11–14).

Moses also regularly felt the piercing and deep knife thrusts of betrayal. Aaron came up with the lame excuse that the golden calf magically appeared on its own (Ex. 32:2, 24), and later he teamed up with Miriam, out of severe envy, and sought to depose Moses (Num. 12:1–9). Two hundred and fifty men joined hands with Korah and viciously opposed Moses because they thought he was an arrogant son-of-a-gun, and afterward some of Moses' most crucial leading men abandoned him (Num. 16). And that was just the tip of the iceberg! We could go on about the day-to-day complexities of the administration that was required in feeding and providing sacrifices for all Israel, or the constant political and military threat and opposition from outsiders, but you get the picture. Moses endured. Would you have given up yet?

Remarkably, even the end of Moses' life was marked by difficulty. Even in his last days he didn't get a reprieve. God announced that he would not let Moses into the Promised Land because he struck a rock rather than speaking to it (Num. 20). God also enabled Moses to see the future of Israel, and it was not full of roses and rainbows—their hardness and rebellion would only continue and worsen. They would be "devoured" and provoke the Lord to anger in such a way that he would abandon them (Deut. 31:17). Moses would see the Promised Land, but not enter it (Deut. 34). Yet Moses endured. He endured a difficult life and a difficult calling for 120 years.

The story of Moses, and perhaps your story, proves Edwards right on his first point—we will face various and innumerable situations and people that will deeply test and sadly try our patience and endurance over and over and over again.

MOSES: SIMULTANEOUSLY JUST AND SINNER

After reminding us of the frequent need for endurance in light of the broken world we live in and the broken people we live with and minister to, Edwards goes on to show the precise nature of long-suffering and how God's love creates the fruit of long-suffering in our hearts.

When we are provoked, he says, we should not seek revenge, but should remain calm and grieve more that their sin is against God than it is against us. Anguish should characterize us more than anger. Our internal disposition, no matter how deep the wound and how constant the hurt, should always be one of love. We should be willing to suffer the loss of our own peace or property rather than defend ourselves or respond in kind. Our love for the incomprehensibly glorious God should make us meek and humble toward others; our love for the immeasurably wise God should make us submit to his sovereign hand, knowing that all things are under his control—even the hurts we endure and the difficulties we walk through. These things come about "by his love and wisdom" and are ordered "justly and even kindly." We should adore his long-suffering toward us and seek to imitate it in our relationships with others. We endure much from them because we love them. We pray for them, because we seek their welfare and long for them to be restored to God and others. If you've endured anything for any amount of time in ministry, does this paragraph sound impossible to you? If you're like me and have even an inkling of self-knowledge when it comes to your heart, you know how impossible that is apart from God's renewing grace in your life.

This is the point where it gets hard, humanly speaking, to believe at times. Moses never *ultimately* gave up. We have no record of Moses dusting off his sandals and running in the opposite direction as far as he could, like a later prophet named Jonah. There is no record of Moses killing a fellow Israelite after months or years of pent-up frustration and anger. Instead, we often see him falling on his face, imploring God, who is slow to anger and abounding in love, to powerfully deliver the Israelites—not only from the Egyptians, but from their own hard hearts. We see him standing in the gap when justice is being meted out, imploring God to stop, so that the nations would know that he really was powerful enough to rescue and redeem such a stiff-necked people. We see him praying for the restoration of Miriam's health right after she sought to overthrow him. When he was reviled, he often did not revile in return, but rather pleaded for God to pour boundless grace into their hearts. It really is true that Moses was one of the most humble men who ever lived.

We might be tempted to think that Moses was so holy that he levitated three inches off the ground and had a constant halo over his head and smile on his face (well, his face did shine for a while!). However, he was a fallen man, constantly in need of grace, compassion, and forgiveness from God. He was a man of contradiction: one moment he was humbly and passionately praying for God to forgive the people who hated him and were trying to kill him, but then he was asking God to take his life or slaughter all the Israelites. In the midst of this tension, Luther's phrase comes in quite handy—*simul iustus et peccator* (at the same time just and sinner).

It's very clear, even from the beginning, that Moses didn't want to accept God's calling. His initial hesitation turned into a pure rejection of God's call, with Moses suggesting to an all-wise God that he should just send someone else. Moses, at times, doubted God's ability to deliver the Israelites. Sometimes he doubted God's faithfulness. When things became too difficult, he said that he would rather die. It wasn't hard for the grumbling of the Israelites to make him a grumbling leader. Unbelief could take over in Moses' heart when he took his eyes off the powerful Rescuer of Israel and focused on the disappointment, discouragement, and difficulty. At times he was self-centered and self-absorbed. There were moments of furious anger and pent-up rage. Surrounded by rebels, Moses too became a rebel and didn't listen to God (Num. 20). Now the story is beginning to be believable. Moses is becoming more human. Maybe he didn't have a halo. Maybe he was just like you and me.

In the final analysis, Moses didn't only respond rightly by long-suffering in the way that Edwards discusses, but also responded in the ways that Edwards warns against: seeking revenge, responding in arrogance and pride, defending oneself, "dealing tyrannically" with others, or even desiring their downfall. By God's grace, Moses had his good days. Because of his sin, he had his bad days. But by God's grace, he did endure, and was ultimately considered faithful as a servant over God's house (Heb. 3:5).

BUT THE QUESTION REMAINS

We are still left with the question: how did Moses endure without calling in a strategic military strike to obliterate everyone or going crazy himself? How do we endure when we've been through hard times, are going through hard times, and will continue to go through hard times?

If time allowed, we might look at the promises that God made when he called Moses, or his constant presence in the pillar of fire and cloud, or his constant provision of food and water. But let's look briefly at what the New Testament has to say, particularly the book of Hebrews: "He endured as seeing him who is invisible" (11:27).

Is that it? Is that the best key to endurance that can be given? Is this a letdown to you? Were you expecting something far more profound? I would suggest that this verse is deeper and more profound than we may initially realize.

According to William L. Lane, the author of Hebrews is claiming that Moses' "fixed habit of spiritual perception," by God's sustaining grace, kept him in the ball game until the end.[4] Another commentator suggests that Moses' "lifelong vision of God was the secret of his faith and perseverance."[5] In other words, the reason our frustration runs so deep, our anger gains so much control, and our endurance dries up so quickly is that we take our eyes off God and his Word and begin to focus on the dust and dirt and the hardness and stubbornness of the situations and people around us. Although we theoretically affirm the truth of the Word and intellectually grasp the reality and presence of God, we begin to live as functional atheists, with God nowhere to be seen in the way we look at things, feel about things, and talk about things. But Moses endured, and you must endure, and I must endure by "seeing him who is invisible." We need the ministry of the Spirit to constantly remind us that God really is working behind the scenes—someone who is infinitely powerful, incredibly wise, and unfathomably loving, and who has a perfect plan that will be executed in his perfect time and in his perfect way. Knowing this doesn't take away the difficult situation or people, nor does it numb any of the real and deep pain that we experience, but it places everything in the context of a world and a ministry and lives that God reigns over in mercy and will one day bring to perfection. Perhaps even now you need to join with me in praying to be filled with the faith that is "the assurance of things hoped for, the conviction of things not seen" (Heb. 11:1).

Even though Moses endured by "seeing him who is invisible," God did make himself audible. God preached a sermon to Moses once, saying

4. William L. Lane, *Hebrews 9–13*, Word Biblical Commentary (Waco: Word, 1991), 376.

5. F. F. Bruce, *The Epistle to the Hebrews*, New International Commentary on the New Testament (Grand Rapids: Eerdmans, 1990), 313.

that he was "merciful and gracious, *slow to anger,* and abounding in steadfast love and faithfulness" (Ex. 34:6–7). But God's patience came to an end when years of constant rebellion and total rejection had turned into decades, and decades into centuries, and centuries into millennia. So what did God do? He became visible in his Son. God's forbearance led him to pass over former sins, but his patience finally came to an end, and his wrath and anger were finally poured out. *on Christ*

The invisible God made himself audible to Moses, but in these "last days" (Heb. 1:1) the audible God became visible in the Word incarnate. They saw him, heard him, and touched him (1 John 1:1–4). It was this visible Word, the Son of God, that God the Father, who is merciful and gracious to us, caused to become sin and to bear the curse, and upon whom he exhausted his furious rage against sin. The God who is slow to anger finally exhausted his wrath on his Son at Calvary, so that he could exercise his grace toward us in whatever calling we have received. Christ is once again invisible to us as he reigns in heaven at the right hand of the Father, but even though we don't see him, we believe in him and rejoice (1 Peter 1:8–9).

A CONCLUDING CHARGE FROM THE APOSTLE PAUL

Paul prays in Colossians 1:11, "May you be strengthened with all power, according to his glorious might, for . . ." For what? Paul is praying for an incredible amount of power for followers of Christ. Why do we need such incredible power, and why does God long to strengthen us with it? Perhaps it's to fly faster than a speeding bullet or jump higher than a skyscraper, or maybe it's to speak really powerfully to people and be a super charismatic and influential leader around the world. But what does Paul actually say? He prays passionately for us to be strengthened "for all endurance and patience" (Col. 1:11). Seriously?! Listen carefully: Paul realizes that we live in a terribly broken world with profoundly broken people. He knows that we will frequently be tempted not to fight the fight and to walk away from the race and from those to whom God has called us to minister. So he prays for our strength to endure. But he not only prays for endurance, but also says that we should be clothed with it (Col. 3:12–14). What Moses endured and what we endure, although painful, shouldn't surprise us. We should rather expect it and be prepared for it by the grace of the gospel. This God-given strength to endure flows to us from the grace purchased for us on Calvary.

I hope you will keep walking on this journey with me. This was just the beginning of the gospel surgery that Jesus put me through that weekend and throughout the first five years of my ministry. In this chapter, I merely wanted to begin by showing something of a worst-case scenario in leadership and by saying that the broken man God called actually endured to the end. In the following chapters, I want to dive deeper into the realities that make us want to quit and the grace that keeps us from doing so. I hope we can keep on walking through these pages with the cry coming from the deepest part of our hearts, "Help me to see, with the eyes of faith, him who is invisible!"

QUESTIONS FOR REFLECTION

1. What are you currently walking through that is testing your endurance? Have you so focused on these things that you have lost sight of the glory of "him who is invisible"?
2. How does the story of Moses' endurance and God's provision of grace for him encourage and strengthen your heart?
3. Read Isaiah 40:29–31. Spend some time in prayer, asking God to strengthen you to be faithful in the midst of what you are presently dealing with.

those who wait / hope on the LORD
1. rise up w/ wings as eagles
2. run & not be weary
3. walk & not faint / give up!

2
EXTERNAL PRESSURES

IN 1963, A CREW of 129 men began a voyage to test the depth range of the newest submarine with the latest technology. Below a safety ship called the *Skylark*, the new submarine, named the USS *Thresher*, circled deeper and deeper, performing "deep dive trials." During the deepest part of the dive, the submarine would descend one hundred feet, radio to the safety ship, and continue its descent. When the submarine came close to what they thought would be the deepest it could go, the *Skylark* received garbled communication that a "minor difficulty" had arisen. That was the last communication heard from anyone just before the submarine imploded due to the enormous external pressure.[1]

In this chapter, that is exactly what I want to focus on—external pressure. While some pressure is obviously to be expected in a church, the examples given below could cause a church leader's heart to feel like disaster might strike at any moment. Our goal in this chapter is to explore some of the external pressures that press in on a leader's heart; the next chapter will deal with the internal idolatries that often exist inside us.

A EXTERNAL PRESSURES

1. Church Conflict

There is more savagery in the book of Judges than in a Steven Segal movie and more bloodshed than Quentin Tarantino could ever imagine. The consequences of everyone doing "what was right in his own eyes" (Judg. 17:6; 21:25) was pretty severe. The entire community was no longer

1. See Norman Palmer, *The Death of the USS Thresher: The Story behind History's Deadliest Submarine Disaster* (Guilford, CT: Lyon's Press, 2004).

moving forward in their mission, but taking the time to slaughter each other in an all-out and constant civil war. There was a new generation that forgot the news of their redemption (2:10), and when there was no king to reign, everyone's selfish desires ruled the day. Would a faithful king come? Ultimately, Jesus did come, but people still drift from the gospel and the consequences are still devastating.

It's interesting to notice what makes the apostle Paul furious. In some passages, Paul is clearly frustrated; in others, he's angry, no doubt—and in all of these for very godly reasons. But in Galatians he's furious—absolutely outraged. Bobby Knight throwing chairs across a basketball court looks like mild disappointment compared to Paul's rage in Galatians. In contrast, the Corinthians were sleeping around, getting drunk at the Lord's Table, and criticizing Paul's seemingly weak ministry, but he still calls them saints and opens his letter with expressions of profound gratitude for God's work in their midst. The leaders in Philippi weren't getting along with each other, many were self-seeking, and some were even preaching the gospel in order to get Paul in more trouble, but he still calls them saints, still gives thanks for God's grace in their lives, and still yearns for them with the affection of Christ Jesus (1:3–8). Although they were an absolute mess, they still roughly understood grace and tried weakly, yet genuinely, to live in light of the gospel. So what on earth made Paul so outraged in Galatians?[2]

They had drifted from the centrality of the gospel. They were biting and devouring one another. Sound familiar? Perhaps Galatians is the New Testament version of Judges.

At the root of all church conflict is either a dilution of the gospel or a subtle drifting away from understanding it and living in light of its implications. Either way, conflict can hurt—really badly. The things that get said in public and in private, the things that are done to secure a certain path or decision, can often be profoundly disappointing and severely disillusioning. Discerning what may be at its root will determine how best to respond. More often than not, it will require gentle, wise, patient, and loving guidance and at times correction and exhortation.[3] It could be something as minor as

2. While Paul was filled with (righteous) anger, he was probably also filled with a deeper anguish of soul (Gal. 4:20). Like the prophets (see Jer. 9:1) and Jesus before him (see Luke 13:34), his soul was greatly disturbed when he saw others not living in dependence upon the sufficiency of God's lavish grace given in Christ.

3. More will be said on dealing with conflict in chapter 7.

someone who is mildly irritating or as major as a churchwide conflict that results in a split. Whatever the cause—and there are an infinite number and variety of causes—conflict will test the mettle of any leader.

Ministry and Family Balance

I knew I was in trouble when my then five-year-old son would wake up in the morning and, if I was actually home, would say, "Bye, Dad." Not "Good morning, Dad" or even "Hey, Dad," but "Bye." I didn't know how to set up boundaries, and I didn't want people to be mad at me or disappointed with me, so I went to every meeting and tried to meet with lots of folks for breakfast. Sometimes it was a busy season, due to heightened tension within the church that required extra meetings, or it was simply me trying to do whatever I thought it would take to grow the church. Sometimes churches have an enormous infrastructure of committees, and sometimes the leadership requires or strongly suggests that the pastor be at each of those meetings. Between moderating and attending meetings, meeting people for counseling, prepping for and teaching Bible studies, attending small groups, listening to people's concerns, getting caught up on e-mails and phone calls, trying to model hospitality within your home, leading a staff, and equipping volunteers, ministry can leave your family with the leftovers.

This is one of the greatest pressure points for any ministry leader and his family.[4] Paradoxically, some pastors disqualify themselves, or get close to disqualifying themselves, from the ministry by being overly involved in ministry and forgetting their first ministry—to their family.

Leadership, Administration, and Management

Much of the training of pastors, especially within my own tradition, is heavily academic and oriented toward the pulpit and teaching ministry.[5] At times, this causes students heading into ministry to think that most, if not all, of their time will be spent preparing lessons or sermons, reading,

---

4. See Bob Burns, Tasha D. Chapman, and Donald C. Guthrie, *Resilient Ministry: What Pastors Told Us about Surviving and Thriving* (Downers Grove, IL: IVP Books, 2013), 199–247.

5. I am not saying this is wrong. Seminaries rightly focus on training leaders who can be about the work of "rightly handling the word of truth" (2 Tim. 2:15). However, more instruction is needed on the more administrative aspects of ministry. Ministerial internships can also help to prepare seminarians for this aspect of ministry.

and meeting others for counseling, discipleship, or evangelism. While larger churches can afford pastors who specialize in various areas of ministry and can provide administrative staff, most pastors find themselves in smaller churches with a significant, if not overwhelming, amount of administrative work to get done.

First, there are the nuances of management that require a lot of time and effort, along with frequent coordination with the skills and availability of many others in the church, such as short- and long-term planning, vision casting and implementation, overseeing various committees, managing conflict, and walking through any programmatic or churchwide shifts. Next, there are the administrative realities of e-mails to respond to, phone calls to return, programs to plan, teachers to find, weekly bulletins to put together, and the church calendar to manage and coordinate with committees or ministry directors. Pastors are often ill-equipped for and unskilled in these things, yet they have to be done for the church to function.[6]

Leadership Isolation

Many pastors confide to others that they and their families often feel very alone and isolated. There is constant reflection and often much disagreement on whether pastors should have close friends in the congregation in which they minister. Either way, a pastor must be extremely cautious and very wise in discerning what burdens to share with whom. A pastor stands in a unique position in giving confidential care to many within the church and dealing with private aspects of larger issues within the ministry. He realizes that there are few, if any, people to whom he can truly and completely unburden his heart.

Another issue is his responsibility to be an example to the flock (1 Peter 5:3). The pressure can feel enormous to have the perfect family, the perfect walk with the Lord, the perfect advice in any situation, and the

6. Resources in this area that I have found useful are Aubrey Malphurs, *Advanced Strategic Planning: A New Model for Church and Ministry Leaders* (Grand Rapids: Baker Books, 2005); *Maximizing Your Effectiveness: How to Discover and Develop Your Divine Design* (Grand Rapids: Baker Books, 2006); Andy Stanley, *Visioneering: God's Blueprint for Developing and Maintaining Vision* (Colorado Springs: Multnomah Books, 1999); David Allen, *Getting Things Done: The Art of Stress-Free Productivity* (London: Penguin Books, 2003); Patrick Lencioni, *The Advantage: Why Organizational Health Trumps Everything Else* (San Francisco: Josse-Bass, 2012); Matt Perman, *What's Best Next: How the Gospel Transforms the Way You Get Things Done* (Grand Rapids: Zondervan, 2014).

appropriate response in every crisis. It often seems hard, if not impossible, to share personal struggles that may be going on in a leader's heart, family, or life. There is often the feeling that one must keep up appearances in order to play the role of pastoral and spiritual leader. Sharing or admitting weaknesses, failures, or temptations may seem like it is definitely not an option, especially in light of the way others have responded in the past when such information was shared.

5. Compassion Fatigue

There are seasons in the life of a pastor when there are enormous demands on his physical and emotional stamina. There are situations where his presence is needed on a regular basis. Families have medical emergencies. Couples need counseling in the midst of an unexpected crisis. Staff members have trouble getting along. A group in the church may be disappointed or upset over a decision.

These are only a few of the incredible amount of things that a pastor is called to enter into, and they can severely deplete the pastor's physical, emotional, and spiritual resources. It is rare that all these things happen at once, but any pastor can attest that there are periods in ministry when one thing comes right after the next, leaving him exhausted and needing significant rest and renewal. Yet such rest is often rare when a leader has to prepare yet another sermon for Sunday and get ready for yet another committee meeting . . . and still have time to be with and minister to his own family.

6. The Unexpected

Things often come up that are totally unexpected and put significant strain on a leader's heart. For example, a local or national economic problem severely impacts the church and weakens its ability to provide financially for its pastor. An exciting new church plant or satellite church comes to town and many families leave. A member gets arrested and the church finds itself in the middle of public scandal. An immediate family member dies or comes down with a life-threatening illness. A crucial core-group member of the plant team quits unexpectedly.

When my wife gave birth to our twin sons, I was extremely excited and knew that I would have a busy season ahead of me. I wasn't expecting that we would almost lose one of them with a severe heart issue. After open-heart surgery on our little guy, we spent almost two weeks in a hospital that was over two hours away. After we were finally able to return home, I knew that my wife would need a tremendous amount of help, now that we had five kids under the age of seven. Thankfully, I'm the lead pastor in a church with multiple pastors and staff and a lot of elders who helped tremendously during that time. However, I was almost entirely absent from the church for almost six months, apart from preaching on most Sundays after we got some rest from the crisis.[7] A smaller church would have a more difficult time surviving such a stint without a pastor and therefore would not have been as flexible or as able to give the necessary support in such a crisis.

Disappointing Results

I counsel many engaged couples who enter into marriage with impossibly high expectations. A few times I have received phone calls only a couple months after the honeymoon, as the couple wanted to come in and discuss their crushing disappointments. I tend to think that married couples are not the only ones who have these kinds of unrealistic expectations. Many pastors enter into ministry, as I did, with the expectation that church members will look forward to their preaching just as much as they look forward to their favorite sitcom, that faithful gospel preaching will *always* lead to significant church growth in a relatively short period of time, that sowing the seed will lead to reaping a harvest of conversions, that their blogs, Twitter feeds, or Facebook posts will be widely quoted and circulated by many who recognize the incredible wisdom the pastor dispenses, and that their church will be the "buzz" around town.

The slow plodding that faithful ministry usually entails can make the pastor impatient or even disillusioned, as expectations are not met and the reality of fallen people living in a sin-cursed world begins to settle in. The discouragement of yet another "down Sunday," when fewer people show up than the week before, the reality of yet another conflict rearing its ugly head, and the thousand other things that can crush our expectations, often make a leader question his call to the ministry.

7. We are grateful that our son, Noah, is doing just fine after major open-heart surgery. A dear friend in the congregation said, "Clay, you've been our pastor for a few years. Now it's time for us to be your pastor." I was simply amazed at our church's response to our family crisis.

Paul's "Anxiety" for All the Churches

Interestingly enough, despite the variety of sufferings and weaknesses that Paul endured, many consider that his "anxiety for all the churches," which was a "daily pressure" on him, was the climax of the burdens that he bore (2 Cor. 11:28).[8] Would the leaders remain faithful? Would the church maintain fidelity to the gospel? Were the pastors training leaders? Was the sick person getting better? Were the widows being visited and served?

Any pastor who knows his congregation well will understand the anxieties that are borne by individuals and couples within the church, as well as by various groups and the church as a whole. A family may be struggling with a significant crisis, a couple may be going through a divorce, a group may be causing division, or a young man may not be able to break his addiction. These are the realities that keep the pastor crying out to God in a simple desire for God to mend broken people and broken things through the power of the gospel.

THEOLOGICAL UNDERPINNINGS—THE FALL AND ITS EFFECT ON WORK

The above realities show that Paul was extremely accurate when he stated that sin and death entered into the world through one man (Rom. 5:12) and that the whole world was "subjected to futility" and remains in "bondage to decay" (Rom. 8:20–21). Sin has disrupted, despoiled, and helped to disintegrate absolutely everything in creation.[9] It perverts and pollutes everything. There is not a single place that you can go to that is not affected by the fall. There is not a single second when you can escape the damage of the fall. There is not a single person, group, church, or community that does not bear the damage caused by the fall. We live in a world that is east of Eden and feels more often like exile in a difficult land than a paradise of pleasure and ease. Pressure is coming from every direction.

This means that, even though you may be in the right vocation or calling, you must still expect to experience frustration in almost everything

---

8. D. A. Carson, *A Model of Christian Maturity: An Exposition of 2 Corinthians 10–13* (Grand Rapids: Baker Books, 2007), 130.

9. See Cornelius Plantinga, *Not the Way It's Supposed to Be: A Breviary of Sin* (Grand Rapids: Eerdmans, 1995), 28–38.

you do.[10] This doesn't mean that we should respond with pessimism or cynicism. Keller writes, "Idealism says, 'Through my work I am going to change things, make a difference, accomplish something new, bring justice to the world.' Cynicism says, 'Nothing really changes. Don't get your hopes up. Do what it takes to make a living. Don't let yourself care too much. Get out of it whatever you can.'"[11] Many ministry leaders begin with the former and endure while significantly infected with the latter. Realism, however, understands precisely what kind of broken world we inhabit and what kind of broken people we serve, while still desiring and expecting God's kingdom to advance through weakness.

This is why we should seek to grow in the "great understanding" that Proverbs 14:29 speaks of: "Whoever is slow to anger has great understanding." It is easy to get angry, easy to get frustrated, easy to lose hope, easy to respond too quickly or harshly. According to the proverb, though, being slow in those things requires "great understanding" that only God can provide. This kind of understanding means that we seek to know God intimately and meditate on his ways faithfully. This is why Psalm 46:1–2 says, "God is our refuge and strength, a very present help in trouble. *Therefore* we will not fear." Notice the order. First, "God is . . ." We begin with theology. Second, "Therefore . . ." From theology we get implications and applications. Knowing who God is as a righteous, holy, sovereign, merciful, loving Lord will lead to the "therefore" of how our hearts should respond to how God has revealed himself and what he claims to have done and to be capable of doing. God has subjected the creation to futility *in hope* (Rom. 8:2); therefore, we should have hope and joy even in the midst of all the brokenness we experience. Consider the time between when God first spoke to Noah and when it first began raining, or between when God promised Moses that his people would enter the Promised Land and when Joshua actually led them there, or between when a Messiah was promised in Genesis 3 and when he came thousands of years later. God, more often than not in Scripture, reveals himself as one who does not mind making us wait; "therefore" we should expect to wait upon our King and be patient.

10. See Tim Keller, *Every Good Endeavor: Connecting Your Work to God's Work* (New York: Dutton, 2012), 94.

11. Ibid., 95.

"Great understanding" also entails knowing ourselves—our temperaments and tendencies. Recent research into pastoral ministry has shown that this is an essential aspect of being faithful and fruitful in ministry. "Pastoral ministry requires learning about ourselves and how we function in various environments and under various circumstances."[12] What kind of situations and people tend to push buttons in our hearts? How do we respond when crises hit? Where, to whom, or to what do we retreat when someone criticizes us? Am I naturally a task-oriented person, needing to strengthen relational skills? Or am I relationally driven, needing to work on administrative abilities? It is crucial to know our strengths and weaknesses, our temperaments and blind spots. We must not only *acknowledge* areas of weakness, but also *address* them as well—seeking the help of others, if necessary.

Finally, knowing others around us and the world we live in is part of possessing "great understanding." Because people are made in God's image, they are capable of some incredible things. Because sin has warped and defiled everyone's heart, people can do and say dreadful and hurtful things. The people and the place that surround us are significantly broken, yet God's power has already broken in, beginning the process of making all things new. Things like this are essential to understand, so that we never think, "I just did a sermon series on that last year, so they shouldn't be struggling with that," or, "I've been in numerous counseling sessions with them, and they still can't see the mess they've created!" A ministry leader with a thoroughly biblical worldview and a thoroughly biblical set of expectations will know that both depravity and dignity will be found, that both brokenness and beauty will be experienced.

C. MAINTAINING INTERNAL BALANCE WHEN THE EXTERNAL PRESSURES ARE TREMENDOUS

Right after the sinking of the USS *Thresher*, the Navy began to make adjustments and alterations to submarine designs and created a new program called SUBSAFE, which was given the oversight of submarine manufacturing. They were tasked to make sure that another

---

12. Burns, Chapman, and Guthrie, *Resilient Ministry*, 107. See especially chaps. 7 and 8.

failure like what they saw with the *Thresher* would never happen again. Sadly, many ministry leaders continue on in ministry with the pressures mentioned above while barely keeping enough internal "pressure" to prevent personal implosion. A vital and affectionate walk with Christ can become nothing but a distant memory, friendships with others who can both confront and care can become almost nonexistent, and physical exhaustion and poor health due to anxiety and stress can put the leader on the brink of disaster. How can this be avoided? At least three things are necessary: a vital walk with Christ, a mentoring relationship with someone who is older and more experienced, and taking care of oneself.

A vital walk with Christ is the first priority. Paul's logic in Ephesians 3:14–19 seems to be that we are "filled with all the fullness of God" as we meditate on "the breadth and length and height and depth" of Christ's love for us. Where do we find out about Christ's love? We find it in the earlier chapters of Ephesians and in the rest of the Bible. Our hearts are filled as we see the glory of Christ's love in the Word. If ministry leaders are going to have "fruit" to offer others in their ministry, they must be trees planted by streams of the living waters of the Spirit, flowing from the heart of Christ in the gospel (see Ps. 1). Regular Bible reading, prayer, and meditation are not things merely to check off in a legalistic scheme, nor are they to be rejected as legalistic; rather, they are the lifeline for our hearts to be sustained in both rainy and dry seasons.[13]

Another significant priority should be to have a mentoring relationship with someone who is older and more experienced. This is vital to stay encouraged, challenged, and refreshed in ministry. The Bible highly recommends seeking counsel from, and having friendships with, those who are wise (Prov. 11:14; 13:20; 24:6). Only a fool thinks that he doesn't need the help, assistance, guidance, and counsel of another (Prov. 12:15). When I was a new believer, someone older and wiser discipled me. When I was thinking about ministry, a pastor regularly counseled and encouraged me. As an intern, assistant pastor, and now senior pastor, I have needed a mentor to help me see what I cannot see,

---

13. See Donald S. Whitney, *Spiritual Disciplines for the Christian Life* (Colorado Springs: NavPress, 1991), 27–64; see also Burns, Chapman, and Guthrie, *Resilient Ministry,* 30–59.

to teach me and help me learn what I do not yet know, to counsel me before messy situations develop, and to encourage or rebuke me after they do. If I am discouraged by what I see, mentors help me focus more on what God has said. If I am overjoyed at something God has done, they rejoice and also remind me that there is work to be done. More than anything else, I am comforted to know that someone knows me deeply and prays for me faithfully.

Finally, taking care of oneself is also a crucial priority for maintaining internal balance in ministry when the external pressure is mounting. Peter Brain defines self-care as "the wisdom to ensure, as far as humanly possible, a wise and orderly work that conserves and lengthens a pastor's ministry."[14] It includes things like getting enough rest and maintaining days off, along with regular exercise and healthy eating habits. As the burdens of ministry grew in my own life, I began to exercise less, sleep less, and eat fast food more, as I was always on the go, usually away from my home and family. I gained fifty pounds, was always tired, could rarely focus, and was irritable. It took way too long for me to realize that I had to change things and set up some boundaries.[15] Only as I took care of myself spiritually and physically would I be most able to serve others faithfully and joyfully over the long haul.[16]

These are only a few of the many things that could be mentioned, but they do provide a place to begin as ministry leaders seek to maintain and grow their internal spiritual balance, so that the external pressures of ministry do not cause yet another casualty. As we move to the next chapter, we'll take a look at how inward idolatry, not external pressure, can sink our hearts.

QUESTIONS FOR REFLECTION

1. Out of all the external pressures mentioned in this chapter, which ones are taking the biggest toll on you right now?

14. Quoted in Burns, Chapman, and Guthrie, *Resilient Ministry*, 60.

15. This "revelation" occurred as I passed out at 13,700 feet with my mentor when we took a hiking trip to Colorado. We came up with a plan afterward about how I would shift my work habits, learn to say no to some things, and eat better. He remains faithful to encourage me in these things. All the more reason to have a faithful mentor!

16. For more on this essential but often missed topic, see Burns, Chapman, and Guthrie, *Resilient Ministry*, chaps. 5 and 6.

2. Which aspects of God's character will provide you with the encouragement you need to respond appropriately to these pressures? His wisdom? His power? His love?

3. Do you strategically plan how you will maintain a vital walk with Christ through meditation on Scripture, prayer, and specific times for reflection? Is there a more experienced ministry leader who could mentor you and encourage you spiritually, and will you contact him soon?

3

WHICH KINGDOM COME?

TONY SAUNDERS was a star baseball player and was drafted in the first round of the major leagues in 1997. He had a unique and much-discussed tattoo on his arm that showed everyone that the game of baseball was everything to him: it had a hand holding a baseball and read "My World." He had dominated the world of baseball since he was a little boy, but one day his world came crashing down. While pitching against the Texas Rangers in 1999, he shattered his arm. After surgery and rehab, he returned, but broke his arm in the first inning upon his return. He was forced to retire at the age of twenty-six.[1] His world crumbled. His entire identity, at that time, was wrapped up in a game, so that when his world crumbled, so did he.

It's very easy for ministry leaders to consider their church or ministry their world. That becomes the place where they find security and satisfaction, acceptance and approval. Such places can become the foundation for building our own kingdoms and making a name for ourselves. Thank God there is another kingdom, a better kingdom, a greater kingdom—the kingdom of God.

What is the kingdom of God like? Thankfully, the kingdom is a major theme in the Bible.[2] For our purposes, let's spend some time in Mark 4, where Jesus explains in a parable what the kingdom of God is like—invisible yet inevitable, insignificant yet incomprehensible:

1. "Tony Saunders," *Wikipedia*, last modified December 10, 2013, en.wikipedia.org/wiki /Tony_Saunders.

2. See Herman Ridderbos, *The Coming of the Kingdom* (Philadelphia: Presbyterian and Reformed, 1962); Geerhardus Vos, *The Teaching of Jesus concerning the Kingdom of God and the Church* (Phillipsburg, NJ: Presbyterian and Reformed, 1979); Graeme Goldsworthy, "Kingdom of God," in *The New Dictionary of Biblical Theology*, ed. T. Desmond Alexander and Brian S. Rosner (Downers Grove, IL: InterVarsity Press, 2000), 615–20.

And he said, "The kingdom of God is as if a man should scatter seed on the ground. He sleeps and rises night and day, and the seed sprouts and grows; he knows not how. The earth produces by itself, first the blade, then the ear, then the full grain in the ear. But when the grain is ripe, at once he puts in the sickle, because the harvest has come." And he said, "With what can we compare the kingdom of God, or what parable shall we use for it? It is like a grain of mustard seed, which, when sown on the ground, is the smallest of all the seeds on earth, yet when it is sown it grows up and becomes larger than all the garden plants and puts out large branches, so that the birds of the air can make nests in its shade." With many such parables he spoke the word to them, as they were able to hear it. He did not speak to them without a parable, but privately to his own disciples he explained everything. (Mark 4:26–34)

THE KINGDOM: INVISIBLE BUT INEVITABLE

It would be wise at the beginning to admit that we have hidden desires and motivations that we don't even know about. Why else would David ask God to uncover his hidden faults or expose unknown sin (Pss. 19:12; 139:23–24)? Only after some painful exposure and because some friends were willing to give me "faithful wounds," do I now know that I entered into ministry with, and continue to struggle against, defining the kingdom according to my own desires and demanding its immediate consummation, rather than defining the kingdom according to God's Word and being patient as it comes.

Because of hidden idolatries and motivations in our heart, we tend to design our kingdom around our heart's desires. So sin defines the "perfect world" on its own terms. A perfect world is where I have my desires fulfilled—now. For the Zealots in Jesus' day, the perfect world was one without Roman rule. They wanted to hear, "The kingdom of God is like a warrior who kills all the Romans—now." So they refused to hear Jesus talk about farmers and seeds. I'm confident that most church leaders have a fairly godly design for the kingdom, because we desire that other people follow Christ and grow in Christ. Yet we often want to press fast-forward on our ministry remote and make people mature faster and our churches grow quicker because we so desperately want these things *now*.

So what is the kingdom of God like for us? Perhaps we might say, "The kingdom of God is like a church planter zealously evangelizing the

44

lost, tirelessly training the found, and passionately growing a megachurch." Or we might say, "The kingdom of God is like a young pastor fearlessly confronting stodgy traditionalism inside the church and hardened unbelief outside the church, becoming so successful that he's asked to do conferences on church revitalization." What do these examples have in common? First, there is a lot of noise. Just look at the enthusiasm, zeal, and excitement! There is also almost immediate gratification—instant impact and sizeable growth. There is frenetic activity, which makes it look like ministry is more like the 100-meter dash than the marathon that requires a steady pace. Finally, the success of the endeavor relies almost completely on the pastor or leader, who eventually becomes a celebrity.

Once we have designed our kingdom according to our desires, we tend to demand its consummation—now. In all likelihood, we have the training, the know-how, the zeal, the insight, the discernment, and the infallible plans to make things happen and to make them happen quickly. There's only one hitch. Ministry includes other people. That simple point demands repeating: ministry includes other people. Other people have their own desires, their own struggles, their own opinions, their own gifts, and their own plans. So we work tirelessly to convince others to accomplish our plans and dreams, convinced that they come from God, convinced that we're building and advancing the kingdom of God. For most of us, though, the kingdom doesn't come in the way we wanted and in the timeframe we expected, which can very often lead to our thinking about leaving a church or leaving the ministry.

If anyone or anything gets in the way of consummating my kingdom or your kingdom, watch out. In our striving to be like God, if others don't enter into my kingdom, they will feel my wrath—now. Perhaps we keep our outward façade of niceness, but inwardly we may be committing murder (Matt. 5:21–22). The result may be an angry outburst of rage, but more often than not, for those in leadership, it is the constant, low-grade frustration, anger, impatience, and coldness, and the constant search for greener grass somewhere else, that deaden our souls, harden our hearts, hurt our families, and threaten our ministry.

This is an often unrecognized and incredibly dangerous place to be in. It is in these moments that we may be tempted (whether we know it or not) to exchange one selfish kingdom for another. Our hearts crave something to find satisfaction in and we will look for it from anyone or anything.[3] Instead of ministry satisfaction, we may go down the path of illicit sexual satisfaction. The tug and pull of pornography or an immoral relationship with another person becomes all the more seductive when our personal kingdom is being crushed. Perhaps it is food, TV, drugs, or alcohol. Whatever it is, our hearts will crave satisfaction and desire it to be found quickly.

At this point, it is life transforming to understand Jesus' teaching on the kingdom. The kingdom is invisible, but its growth is inevitable. Jesus begins by saying, "The kingdom of God is like a farmer"—not like a warrior, not like a CEO, not like a movie star, but like a farmer. It's not often that you see a farmer being interviewed on TV, and not too many people are eager to hear what a farmer has to say. More often than not, as we and our loved ones sit to eat breakfast, lunch, and dinner, as we wear the clothes that we wear, and enjoy many other things that begin in the fields of a farmer, we are not inclined to think about him or her and probably less inclined to be envious about a job that requires such long hours and often unnoticed and unthanked work.

But let me share where my heart begins to long for what the farmer has in the parable. "He sleeps and rises night and day" (Mark 4:27). While working diligently and faithfully, the farmer knows that the seed (invisible as it rests under the earth) has the power to grow on its own, along with the help of some good weather. The farmer is responsible to fulfill his task, but the growth of the seed and the size of the harvest ultimately depend on circumstances outside his control.

The farmer works and rests while the seed grows gradually (v. 28). We tend to desire that our kingdoms come immediately, whereas Jesus teaches that God's kingdom will come gradually. Growth is happening under the soil, even if you cannot see it. Growth is occurring in the plant, even if it is so slow that you do not notice it. So it is in Jesus' kingdom, and so it should be in our expectations. Many have read Scripture through many

3. See Tim Keller, *Counterfeit Gods: The Empty Promises of Money, Sex, and Power, and the Only Hope That Matters* (New York: Dutton, 2009); Dan B. Allender and Tremper Longman, *Breaking the Idols of the Heart: How to Navigate the Temptations of Life* (Downers Grove, IL: InterVarsity Press, 2007); Elyse Fitzpatrick, *Idols of the Heart: Learning to Long for God Alone* (Phillipsburg, NJ: P&R Publishing, 2001); G. K. Beale, *We Become What We Worship: A Biblical Theology of Idolatry* (Downers Grove, IL: InterVarsity Press, 2008).

times and can quote verses on the reality and progressiveness of ministry, and yet when we hit snags or experience setbacks, or when things move forward only at a snail's pace, we are disappointed and frustrated. When those times come, Jesus could say, "I told you so," but he doesn't. Instead, his Spirit encourages us to wait and see. *Be still & know HE sustains Ps. 54 & 46 10 I AM God*

The growth of the kingdom is almost invisible. Sometimes it occurs where we can't see it, and sometimes the growth is so slow that we miss it. But this text also shows that the growth of the kingdom is inevitable (v. 29). The harvest will come in God's timing and in his way. There will be fruit to enjoy. There will be food to satisfy. While God uses us as instruments in his kingdom, the growth of the kingdom isn't ultimately dependent on us; it is dependent on what Christ has done for us and continues to do for us by the work of the Spirit in us and through us. We can rest and sleep when it is night and work while it is day, because we know that the seed of the word has the power in itself to expand God's kingdom, not mine.

THE KINGDOM: IT SEEMS INSIGNIFICANT, BUT BECOMES INCOMPREHENSIBLE

When I was in high school and college, I would take friends from Indiana to hike, climb, and raft in Colorado. When we hit Kansas, we would see signs that said, "See the world's largest prairie dog!" A few more miles down the I-70, another sign would say, "Fifteen-foot prairie dog!" The next sign would say, "You have to see it to believe it!" Overcome with the need to see and experience something so extraordinary, we eventually stopped to check it out. Suffice it to say (although we inwardly knew this would be the case!) that the real thing left much to be desired. We left deflated and disappointed, especially when we found out our furry friend was made out of concrete.

On a much more serious note, I think Jesus is talking about deception and perception in this text. When we think about the kingdom, our hearts tend to be drawn to things and people and experiences that *seem* to be powerful, *seem* to be meaningful, and *seem* to be satisfying, but in the end they leave us empty, disappointed, and deflated. Our hearts are so easily deceived in pursuing a kingdom that is the creation of our own desires—just read the newspapers and watch the news, and you'll see many celebrities who have said, "There's got to be more than this." Even as pastors, whether

47

we've achieved what we wanted or not, we can say, "There's got to be more than this." When our kingdoms collapse and our dreams are shattered, it's often the mercy of God, not the judgment of God, calling us back to what alone is truly satisfying and truly motivating.[4]

In this parable, Jesus proclaims that there is something more and that we rarely see it. In fact, it seems imperceptible. It's the size of a mustard seed, the smallest known seed of the time. It seems weak, it seems unsatisfying, and it seems like it isn't worth your while. But Jesus says, "Watch it grow." Although its beginnings are almost imperceptible, its conclusion will be incomprehensible (Mark 4:32). We cannot now fully comprehend the fullness of its power, the enormity of its significance, the broadness of its impact, nor the depth of its satisfaction for all who will come near. Jesus is helping us move from deception to perception, so that we can rightly "see through" to the deeper reality of the kingdom of God. It may look weak and powerless, but it is strong and advancing; it may look foolish and incompetent, but it is wise and masterful; it may look frustrating and disappointing, but it is deeply satisfying and soul refreshing.

Leave the I-70 and travel along Highway 24 from Colorado Springs to Buena Vista, Colorado. Just about two miles outside of that little town, in the middle of the mountains, there is a small, rusty, bullet-riddled sign that says "Overlook .2 miles." The road is not paved, there are rocks that must be driven around, and there is quite a bit of trash and even a port-a-potty at the turnoff. But if you're willing to drive a little bit and get your car dusty, you'll end up with one of the greatest views in North America as you stand on the edge of a valley directly across from the Collegiate Peak Range with nine mountains towering over 14,000 feet high, glistening with snow on moonlit evenings. *Breathtaking* doesn't even begin to describe it. The questionable beginning at the turnoff ends with an awe-inspiring view that convinces you that the journey to get there has been well worth it.

In this parable, Jesus is wisely teaching his disciples—and pastors today—what to expect and what to hope and long for. The kingdom of God may look weak, compared to the kingdoms of this world. The kingdom of God, at times, may seem to offer things that are less satisfying than the immediate pleasures that the kingdoms of this world have to offer. Yet one

---

4. See Amos 4; see also Larry Crabb, *Shattered Dreams: God's Unexpected Pathway to Joy* (Colorado Springs: Waterbrook, 2001).

day everything hidden will be revealed. The kingdom of God will come on earth as it is in heaven. This is why the crucial teaching of the already and not-yet of the kingdom of God is so important. It tempers your expectations for the present and whets your appetite for the more that is to come.

IDOLATRY: AGAIN

In his early years, Theodore Roosevelt traveled to Europe with his family. On one trip, they went hunting for a few days, but Roosevelt couldn't hit a thing. He later wrote:

> One day they read aloud an advertisement in huge letters on a distant billboard, and I then realized that something was the matter, for not only was I unable to read the sign but I could not even see the letters. I spoke of this to my father, and soon afterwards got my first pair of spectacles, which literally opened an entirely new world to me. I had no idea how beautiful the world was until I got those spectacles. I had been a clumsy and awkward little boy, and while much of my clumsiness and awkwardness was doubtless due to general characteristics, a good deal of it was due to the fact that I could not see *and yet was wholly ignorant that I was not seeing.*[5]

Idols make us blind. They not only make us blind, but also make us blind to our blindness. As many have noted, idolatry often turns good things into god things, where we seek ultimate satisfaction or security. I am not saying that every pastor who reads this is, right now, committing idolatry. I am saying, alongside men like Calvin, who said that our hearts are idol-making factories, that ministry idols can be and are a regular temptation for those in vocational ministry. *"seek those things "above" where Christ is!*

Colossians 3:1–10 is a great passage of Scripture to give us new "spectacles" to understand what is going on inside our hearts. To the extent that Christ is not supreme and preeminent in our hearts and lives, and to the extent that we are not seeking the things that are above, something else will be preeminent and our hearts will seek things here below. This is why it is so crucial for ministry leaders not only to feed others with the glory of Christ and the wonder of grace, but also to nourish their own souls at the

---

5. Quoted by Edmund Morris, *The Rise of Theodore Roosevelt* (New York: Random House, 2001), 34 (emphasis added).

feet of him who is the fountain of life. This is one of the reasons why Paul says that covetousness is idolatry (3:5). We are seeking life and fullness in someone or something other than God.

Keep this in mind: covetousness always says "more!" and never says "enough!" However, when the gospel of Christ and the glory of God capture our hearts, and when we see the supremacy of Christ and rest in his sufficiency, hearts that are content in the gospel will always say "enough!" and never say "more!"

Because I struggle with this idolatry in my heart, and I venture you do too, I am often tempted and often succumb to thinking like this: "I know I have Jesus, but I'd be happier if more people were sitting in the pews, if more people were grateful for what I do, if more people gave so we could have a larger budget or build a larger building, so that I could have more of a reputation and be known and admired by more people." More. More. More. During the times when I am not sinking my heart deep into the "It is finished" of the gospel, I long for more, am never satisfied, and never say "enough." What is the "I'd be happier if . . ." of your heart? Seriously. Take a moment and reflect on that question.

Reflection is important because ministry leaders make such enormous sacrifices for their idols, whatever they may be. All idols demand that we sacrifice in order that they will bless us, so in order to experience the blessing of recognition, power, comfort, control, acceptance, or any other idol, we sacrifice our health, our families, our relationships, and even our own walk with Christ. This is why, I believe, when we are pursuing the idols that promise more and always deliver less, we will be filled with the anger and lying and bad-mouthing of others that Paul describes in verses 8–9.

The consequences of this idol worship are that, deep down, leaders may be filled with anger or constant disappointment with others because they are not able to deliver what the leader is looking for. The consequences for the leader are a dry and hard heart toward the Lord and often wrecked health and strained relationships with other leaders, with other people in the congregation or ministry, and even with his own wife and children. Idols subtly bring death into practically every sphere of life.

If the idols we are pursuing are blessing us, we will feel alive and successful—and prideful. If the idols we are pursuing are cursing us, we will feel despair and death. In the moments (and there have been way too many) when I have thought about leaving the ministry, the Lord has usually been quick to point out that I have been building my own kingdom and pursuing false gods. The disappointment and discouragement that I have felt has been more about my reputation being hurt and my selfish kingdom being crushed than about genuinely feeling I wasn't called to ministry. I have realized that I have needed to repent for acting like some kind of Pharaoh and forcing the lambs under my watch and care to work hard to build Clay Werner's kingdom, rather than prayerfully advance God's. It's as if God has been saying, "Clay, let my people go!"

Here's what I want to say: when you realize that your internal idolatry is driving your heart and ministry, you don't change by mere willpower. *Moving forward isn't about sin management, but about worship realignment.* Deep down, at your core, Christ must become more satisfying than anything and everything else. Thankfully, the Spirit is eager and willing to help reveal Christ to your heart in such a way that you'll treasure Christ above all things and endure even when the kingdom of God around you seems so weak and slow.[6]

THE KINGDOM OF GOD REMAINS FOREVER

Kingdoms come and kingdoms go, but the kingdom of God will remain forever. The danger of ministry is that pursuing our own kingdom can be easily disguised by using language from the kingdom of God.[7] Too often, leaders themselves are blind to the reality that they are making ministry "their world" rather than a place of nourishment for God's people and equipping for God's mission. However, once the little kingdom is forsaken and repented of, the kingdom of God that is invisible yet inevitable, seemingly insignificant but yet incomprehensible in its power and breadth, will provide the deepest joy and the greatest security, especially as the eyes of our hearts remain fixed on its King.

6. Some helpful material for diagnosing idolatry are David Powlison's "X-Ray Questions" in *Seeing with New Eyes: Counseling and the Human Condition through the Lens of Scripture* (Phillipsburg, NJ: P&R Publishing, 2003), 129–44; Dan B. Allender and Tremper Longman, *The Cry of the Soul: How Our Emotions Reveal Our Deepest Questions about God* (Colorado Springs: NavPress, 1994). I have also found John Owen's books *Communion with God, Meditations on the Glory of Christ,* and *On Being Spiritually Minded* very helpful in cultivating a heart of worship and adoration.

7. See Paul David Tripp, *A Quest for More: Living for Something Bigger Than You* (Greensboro, NC: New Growth Press, 2007), 72–82.

QUESTIONS FOR REFLECTION

1. If you spent a season praying for God to reveal your "hidden faults" (Ps. 19:12) and to test your heart and thoughts (Ps. 139:23–24), what might be motivating you at the deepest level?
2. If you were to describe your perfect kingdom, what would it be like? How would you answer the question, "I'd be happy if . . . ?"
3. How does a biblical understanding of the kingdom temper your expectations for your current ministry situation and context?

4

THE GIFT OF DISILLUSIONMENT

ON NOVEMBER 29, 1981, a 160-foot crabbing boat named *St. Patrick* set out with a crew of eleven men into the Gulf of Alaska. During its first night at sea, the crew encountered an incredible storm that generated ninety-mile-per-hour winds and seventy-foot waves. The boat could not be steered, and almost all the lights were knocked out by the waves. Finally, it happened. One wave was large enough to make the entire boat rock completely onto its side. After a few moments, when the boat did not right itself, the skipper gave the command to abandon ship. The eleven members of the crew tied themselves together with a rope and jumped into the near-freezing water in the middle of the night, hoping to survive.[1]

It doesn't take long, after experiencing a major storm in leadership, for you to begin to wonder if you need to abandon ship. Whether it's seventy-foot waves or just an extremely slow leak in nice weather, there are times when walking away from the community to which God has called you to minister seems to be safer than staying put.

It was after multiple times of standing on the edge and looking into the water that I realized something: Genesis 3 really happened. I'm not saying I didn't know the content of that chapter in my Bible. I just think that I, like many others, didn't fully grasp the profound implications of what it reveals about the world we live in and the people we are called to serve. Simply put, everything is broken.

At this point, it is wise to bring on Francis Schaeffer and Dietrich Bonhoeffer as part of our crew. With far more experience in far greater

---

1. Spike Walker, *Working on the Edge: Surviving in the World's Most Dangerous Profession* (New York: St. Martin's Press, 1991), 251–70.

storms than you and I have seen or probably ever will see, they can help us navigate in these rough waters, while pointing us to a deeper understanding of the truth.

OUR COMMUNITY IS NOWHERE CLOSE TO HEAVEN

As leaders committed to the historic Reformed faith, we regularly and passionately proclaim the truth about depravity: people are dead in sin (Eph. 2:1–2), and their hearts are desperately wicked (Jer. 17:9) apart from God's gracious work in them. Yet I've seen in others, and especially in my own heart, a significant lack of wisdom when it comes to understanding these truths and applying them to our everyday lives and everyday relationships. I think many of us walk around having functionally forgotten Genesis 3 ever happened, and then we find that people do not live up to our expectations and desires for them.

Most of us in leadership have fairly godly desires for others. We long for people to follow Christ and grow in him. But these good desires can turn vicious when we unconsciously expect people to live now only like they'll be able to in heaven—perfectly. The community our hearts often desire is a community of people that never disappoint us, rarely show the effects of sin in their lives, make serving in the church easy, and make us laugh a lot. In the words of Eugene Peterson, "The church we want becomes the enemy of the church we have."[2]

When we do not understand the far-reaching implications of the fall and the deep-rootedness of sin in the human heart, we can do great harm to relationships.[3] "If we demand, in any of our relationships, either perfection or nothing, we will get nothing."[4] To whatever extent we unconsciously minimize the reality of sin, we will idealize our picture of the church and remain regularly disappointed, frustrated, and angry. Our conscious or unconscious expectations are so high that there is no one or no church that can possibly live up to them.

This is why diving deep into the Bible's concept of the church as the community of God's people is so vital and practical for anyone ministering

---

2. Eugene Peterson, *Practice Resurrection: A Conversation on Growing Up in Christ* (Grand Rapids: Eerdmans, 2010), 29.

3. *The Complete Works of Francis A. Schaeffer* (Wheaton: Crossway, 1982), 3:28–30.

4. Ibid., 30.

5 Languages of love

to anybody in this broken world. Knowing these things can reorient our internal compass more toward reality.

Think of the church as the community of God's people. The patriarchal families were often tearing each other apart. Israel was torn in two. The disciples argued about who was going to be the greatest among them, and the early church was wracked with immorality, idolatry, and heterodoxy that constantly threatened its vitality. Francis Schaeffer explains that in Scripture, God goes out of his way to expose the weakness and depravity of believers in order to deflate the "utopian concept" of community that many carry around in their hearts. And yet, somehow, when we reach a stretch of rough water in leadership, we're often caught unprepared.

Remarkably, Bonhoeffer jumps to our side and claims that the raging winds and high waves are a gift. He says that God, as an act of grace, shatters our idealistic and romanticized version of what people should be like. *If we are fortunate*, Bonhoeffer declares, we will be "overwhelmed by great disillusionment with others," and the sooner this can happen the better.[5] It is here that the apostle Paul can help us. In Colossians 3, he gives us a realistic portrait of what life will be like for leaders in the church that Jesus purchased with his own blood. In verse 11, Paul names all the various groups of people whom God has called into his one church—Greeks, Jews, circumcised, uncircumcised, slave, free. God didn't create multiple churches for each group, but one church for the multiple groups. They were called to be one and to maintain the unity that the Spirit had already wrought (Eph. 2:15; 4:3).

OUR COMMUNITY IS THE PLACE WHERE GOD TRANSFORMS US

In John 15, Jesus tells the disciples to love one another. Jesus isn't being sentimental. He is giving them a charge. Remember, Jesus defines love in verse 13 as willing self-sacrifice for another, and this is what makes living life together so difficult.[6] The difficulty of loving comes from the disciples' differences and inherent depravity: one was a Zealot (an extremely devout Jew, who cared enormously about purity), one was a tax collector (whom

5. Dietrich Bonhoeffer, *Life Together: The Classic Exploration of Faith in Community*, trans. John W. Doberstein (San Francisco: Harper and Row, 1954), 26–27.

6. Paul David Tripp, *Broken Down House: Living Productively in a World Gone Bad* (Wapwallopen, PA: Shepherd Press, 2009), 163–76.

all Jews hated and despised), others were fisherman (I bet they smelled like fish—all the time!), and two were called the Sons of Thunder because of how eager they were to call down judgment on others. The Gospels portray the disciples as men who were constantly arguing, complaining, and doubting. It is precisely *those kinds of people* that Jesus says to love.

If we return to Paul's comments in Colossians 3:11, we see that he too understands the great differences among those who comprise the community of the church. Many of these groups, out of a sense of individual and collective superiority, actually hated each other and wanted to keep far away from each other. Here is where the incredible news comes in. Paul is telling the Colossians and all of us, "Look. You see those people that you might naturally despise or even hate? You see those people who make life difficult for you, who are different from you, who disappoint you, and who hurt you? You see those people who are bruised and broken? In the sight of God, because they have faith, they are 'chosen, holy, and dearly beloved.' God doesn't just put up with them—he cherishes them. God sees their yuck, but because of Christ he considers them holy. Though there isn't anything inherently loveable in them, they are still dearly loved." And Paul isn't just describing "them"—he is describing us.

In other words, Paul is charging us believers to have a "God's-eye view" of those we are called to minister to. If that is how God sees them, then that is how we should see them. We shouldn't see them as problems or projects or as obstacles preventing us from getting what we really want, because if we do, we'll tend to seek refuge in self-protective isolation or play favorites. It's so easy for pastors to stay busy reading and studying and not interacting with people. It's so easy to keep the door to our office and the door to our heart shut. It's so easy to keep conversations short and not really spend time deeply entering into the life of another. It's so easy to commit, knowingly or unknowingly, to minister only to the people who affirm you, who make you feel good, and who have few problems. If you've done any of these things, it's time to come out of hiding and to pursue messy people with messy problems and messy hearts.

We should see the people right in front of us as "chosen, holy, and dearly beloved." *This* is the context in which God has called us to serve. *This* is the reality into which he has called us to enter. *These* are the kinds of people with whom we will interact on a daily basis. When we have community amnesia, we will jump ship. When we remember *divorce* the reality of depravity and the grace of our and their identity, we will cherish and be patient with the community in which God has graciously placed us.

THE PROCESS OF GROWTH IS JUST THAT—A PROCESS

Immediately following Paul's teaching on the identity of the people who make up the community in which we live, he tells us to put on a new suit of clothes, purchased for us through the life, death, and resurrection of Christ. What do these clothes consist of? "Compassion, kindness, humility, meekness, and patience, bearing with one another and, if one has a complaint against another, forgiving each other; as the Lord has forgiven you, so you also must forgive. And above all these put on love, which binds everything together in perfect harmony" (Col. 3:12–14).

Paul, again, is not being sentimental. We can't look at this passage and say, "Wow, if only they made a hallmark card like that!" Paul is being radically truthful about the kinds of clothes we have to wear to survive living with other people (and what they should wear to survive us!). If we're going to survive the harsh reality of high winds and enormous waves while crab fishing in Alaska, then we had better wear survival suits. Paul is giving us his own version of the survival suit when he explains what to put on when we walk into the lives of fellow sinners.

Compassion is the inward heart of sympathetic concern for others. Others will have material, psychological, relational, and spiritual issues in their lives that should elicit compassion from our heart more than frustration. *Kindness* is the outward and concrete expression of compassion toward someone in need. Rather than having a what-can-I-get-out-of-this-relationship mentality, gospel clothing calls us to be more concerned with giving in order to alleviate someone else's need. *Humility* is thinking rightly *of* ourselves as sinners saved by grace and also not thinking *about* ourselves too much. In community, when we see the mess and problems and sin in someone else's life, it's easy to be overcome by an unconscious sense of superiority. Just think of the messes that Paul saw in the churches and the people he interacted with, and yet he genuinely considered himself the chief of sinners! *Meekness* has been defined as "the quality of not being overly impressed by a sense of one's self-importance" [7] and being "considerate of others; willing to waive one's rights." [8] How often does our impatience and frustration come as a result of others not respecting us as we think they should or an unwillingness to consider someone else more important than ourselves?

Next is where Paul really upsets me. I don't want to admit that he is right. I'd rather spend my whole life trying to find a place not affected by the fall than submit to what he says. But I must. *Patience* is not about waiting for the doctor or for the cars to move in the drive-through so I can finally get my long-awaited double cheeseburger. Patience is *perseverance under provocation*. It is being slow to anger, just like God. It could be thousands of years before God's wrath is poured out at the last judgment. And yet, if others cross my kingdom, they feel my wrath—now. My anger and impatience too often have a hair trigger. Yet Paul says that God, in an act of mercy and transforming grace, is placing us squarely in the middle of a community that will regularly disappoint us or provoke us to anger, and so we must consciously put on patience. And the apostle goes further: *bearing with one another* and *forgiving one another*. Notice that the "one another" are Christians! Paul is saying that others will make decisions we don't agree with, say things we don't like, and do things that might hurt us, so we must be ready to bear with them and be ready to forgive. The verb tense implies that this will need to take place regularly and continuously! This is why Peter says, "Love covers a multitude of sins" (1 Peter 4:8). He is graciously telling us ahead of time that God will provide numerous opportunities to learn the gracious response of forbearance and forgiveness.

Paul is reminding us that the process of gospel growth is painstakingly slow and lifelong. This is why I find it fascinating that most of the imagery in Scripture that reveals the nature of change is organic. Crops and other plants don't grow overnight; they take time and require patience. So does ministering to people-in-process while we are in that same process. We tend to desire a more perfect community to minister to and people who are being transformed more quickly than they currently are. Too often, if the community doesn't display gospel character the way I think it should and

7. Frederick W. Danker, *A Greek-English Lexicon of the New Testament and Other Early Christian Literature*, 3rd ed. (Chicago: University of Chicago Press, 2000), 861.
8. Ibid.

isn't changing at the pace I would like, I tend to consider jumping ship. This is when Bonhoeffer counsels us to be more filled with gratitude than the urge to jump:

> A pastor should not complain about his congregation, certainly never to other people, but also not to God. A congregation has not been entrusted to him in order that he should become its accuser before God and men . . . . [The pastor] had better examine himself first to see whether the trouble is not due to his wish dream that should be shattered by God; and if this be the case, let him thank God for leading him into this predicament.[9]

With whatever you have gone through or are going through, is your heart filled with compassion, humility, and meekness? Are your interactions with fellow sinners marked by kindness, patience, and forgiveness? If we are honest, if we let these questions penetrate deep enough, we'll find that we need grace just as much as, if not more than, the people we were pointing our fingers at.

OUR COMMUNITY IS A GIFT OF LOVING GRACE AND THE CONTEXT OF TRANSFORMING GRACE

I hear it said way too often that ministry would be great if it weren't for the people. I understand that most are joking when they say it, but I also tend to think that they partly mean it. But Scripture is very clear that the context of change, not only for the people you may lead, but also for yourself, is the sinner-filled community that I described above.[10] In fact, Christians who are much farther along in this process than I currently am, charge us to consider this very community as a gift of God's grace.[11] Why?

To begin with, this is the place where others will be instruments of grace for you. Though they will do so imperfectly, some will speak encouraging words to you. Some will pray for you. Some may correct you, if needed (and even when not necessary!). Some will use Scripture to give you strength and speak into your life at an opportune time. Some will show you what forgiveness looks like when you fail. Some will amaze you by their

9. Bonhoeffer, *Life Together*, 29–30

10. See Wayne Grudem, *Systematic Theology* (Grand Rapids: Zondervan, 1994), 756.

11. Bonhoeffer, *Life Together*, 30.

faith during difficult times, and you will learn by their grace-driven endurance. When I went to the mountains to pray about leaving the ministry, as I mentioned in chapter 1, I listened to a sermon by C. J. Mahaney.[12] He made a point that changed my life and left me in tears. He said that too often pastors see only areas of deficiency in their people and not evidences of grace, and therefore they become bitter and joyless. I was one of those pastors, and I prayed and prayed that God would help me see more of his work in his people's lives. When I came back, I marveled at all the ways in which people in the church had ministered to me and my family, and I hadn't even noticed. The community I was in and the community you are in are God's instruments of grace to transform us, and we are instruments of grace to help transform them. "Maybe the church as we have it provides the very conditions and proper company congenial for growing up in Christ, for becoming mature, for arriving at the measure of the stature of Christ. Maybe God knows what he is doing, giving us church, this church."[13]

It is equally true that God will use this community to expose the heart-idols in your life. "One of the great things about living as part of a community is that in community people walk all over your idols. People press your buttons. . . . And that gives us opportunities to spot our idolatrous desires."[14] If you find yourself getting angry at someone or because of some situation, ask yourself why. If you find yourself despairing over someone or because of some situation, ask yourself why. If you find yourself extremely joyful, ask yourself why. Are they threatening to take away something you cherish? Are they blocking something you adore? I realized early on that I have a significant idol of comfort. Constant conflict made me seek comfort anywhere I could find it, especially in a quiet office with a closed door in the safety of reading books. I could always use the pastoral excuse that I was studying. Because phone calls and e-mails made me nervous, I began to avoid answering, making the excuse that I was extremely busy. I also sought comfort from food. I couldn't control people or circumstances, but

12. C. J. Mahaney, "Sustaining a Pastor's Soul," sermon preached in Louisville, Kentucky, at the Together for the Gospel Conference. You can listen to this sermon at "Sustaining the Pastor's Soul," *C.J.'s View from the Cheap Seats* (blog), September 9, 2008, http://www.sovereigngraceministries.org/blogs/cj-mahaney/post/2008/09/09/Sustaining-the-Pastore28099s-Soul.aspx.

13. Peterson, *Practicing Resurrection*, 14. See also Tim Chester and Steve Timmis, *Total Church: A Radical Reshaping around Gospel and Community* (Wheaton: Crossway, 2008), 113.

14. Tim Chester, *You Can Change: God's Transforming Power for Our Sinful Behavior and Negative Emotions* (Wheaton: Crossway, 2010), 155.

I could control not feeling bad physically, so I would make sure I never felt hungry. That would be one less uncomfortable thing I had to worry about in the midst of all that was going on. Fifty pounds later, I realized I had a problem! As the idols in my heart were exposed, I realized the gospel needed to go much deeper into my heart.

Further, God will use the community you are in to reveal his glory to you. John Newton often wrote letters to a man by the name of John Ryland, who went through some fairly severe conflicts in the church to which he was ministering.[15] To summarize much of what Newton said, it is often the case that the times of greatest difficulty can often bring about the moments of greatest intimacy with Christ. It is in the moments of weakness that we depend on his strength. It is in the moments of confusion that we trust in his wisdom. It is in the moments of heartache that we trust the "infallible Pilot"[16] who is at the helm of the ship and is using his infinite love, incomprehensible wisdom, and insurmountable power to bring about his glorious purposes, no matter where we are and whom we are with.

These three things are by no means an exhaustive list of the reasons why God places us where he does, but they are a beginning, and they leave room for much more thought and meditation. The community you are in is broken far worse than you could ever imagine, but God is in the process, even though it is slow, of making all things new. This requires great patience on the part of any and all who would lead in the church. The community you are in is the very place in which God has graciously put you in order to conform you to the image of his Son. This should cause deep gratitude in your heart.

YOU DON'T HAVE TO ABANDON SHIP

After twenty hours in the water, the crewmen from the *St. Patrick* were finally found by the Coast Guard. Two were still alive. The other ten didn't make it. After a few days in intensive care, the surviving crewmen were placed in the same hospital room. The first one said, "I never would have believed that a ship like the *St. Patrick* would have gone under as quickly as she did!" Bob Kidd, the other deckhand, quietly responded,

15. You can find these letters in *Wise Counsel: John Newton's Letters to John Ryland, Jr.*, ed. Grant Gordon (Carlisle, PA: Banner of Truth Trust, 2009).

16. Ibid., 93; see also p. 164.

"Wally, it didn't go down. It didn't sink. They found the ship floating the day after we abandoned it. They're towing it in right now."[17]

What happened to that crew was awful, yet it is also instructive. The ship was strong and more stable than they thought, and they shouldn't have jumped off. Perhaps you want to abandon ship. Perhaps you think that there is no way you or those around you will make it. But God promises that he will not abandon what he has begun (Phil. 1:6; Heb. 13:5). He will not abandon you, and he may just use you to turn the ship right side up—in his way and in his timing, of course.

QUESTIONS FOR REFLECTION

1. How do you respond to others when they hurt or disappoint you? Do you regularly ask God to help you "put on" the clothing Paul mentions in Colossians 3?

2. How has God used the community you serve to uncover idols in your life?

3. In what ways has God revealed his glory to you in the midst of the community you serve? *testing to produce faith*

17. Walker, *Working on the Edge*, 269–70.

5

IF THE RESURRECTION AIN'T TRUE, I'M GONNA GET BLITZED!

PRIOR TO THE 1976 football season, each member of the Tampa Bay Buccaneers spent ten weeks of exhausting two-a-day workouts in the brutal South Florida heat. The practices were so intense that some of the players were unable to play when the season began. During the season, their "sidelines looked like a Civil War infirmary," and the team was replacing hurt players with men from the Canadian Football League and even from off the street.[1] At the end of the season, with a record of 0–14, twenty-one players were on injured reserve and eighteen had knee surgery. After the final game, the players were ready to call it quits: "The lot was full of loaded U-Hauls, station wagons with bulging luggage racks, pickups hauling flatbed trailers heaped with furniture and other household stuff. *The diaspora couldn't be accomplished quickly enough.*"[2] *problems / issues*

I wonder if you can make any connection between that story and either your story or the story of someone you know in ministry. It's no wonder that people who are exhausted from countless gatherings or beat up and bullied around can't wait to pack their bags and drive away. Stay injured long enough, stay exhausted long enough, watch others "succeed" long enough when you feel like you are losing, and eventually you might walk away from the sideline and leave the ministry—or even worse, the faith.

You are not alone.

1. Pat Toomay, "A Debilitating Case of Bucs Fever," ESPN.com, accessed March 15, 2012, http://espn.go.com/page2/s/toomay/011227.html (emphasis added).
2. Ibid.

Peter Abelard, the twelfth-century theologian, was thrown into despair over his experiences with other Christians. He once wrote to a friend that he thought that every ecclesiastical assembly had been convened to condemn him: "Often, God knows, I fell into such a state of despair that I thought of quitting the realm of Christendom and going over to the heathen, there to live a quiet Christian life among the enemies of Christ at the cost of what tribute was asked."[3] In a letter to Melanchthon, after feeling beaten "black and blue" by Luther himself, Calvin wrote, "When I reflect how much, at so unseasonable a time, these . . . quarrels divide and tear us asunder, I almost entirely lose courage."[4]

Not long after Francis Schaeffer moved to Switzerland, he went through a major spiritual crisis. He had seen so much political maneuvering and division at the denominational level, and so much biting and devouring among Christians at the congregational and personal level, that he couldn't quite understand how the claims of Christianity could be true in light of such brokenness in the church. Not only that, he had also hoped to be further along in his own walk with Christ, and was discouraged and depressed at his own lack of progress in spiritual growth. Was Christ truly the Redeemer? Had the Spirit truly been poured out in power? He began to question everything about Christianity.[5]

Even in my own life and ministry, I had seen so much in others and in my own heart that I genuinely began to wrestle with the veracity of Christianity. Summing up everything that has been discussed so far, the combination of external difficulties, inward idolatries, and a theology that is not being lived with a heart-level functionality can often lead to questions about your call to ministry or even confusion about the truthfulness of Christianity. What are some of the specific things that can lead to these doubts?

3. Quoted in Os Guinness, *God in the Dark: The Assurance of Faith beyond a Shadow of Doubt* (Wheaton: Crossway, 1996), 132.

4. Ian M. Tait, "Calvin's Ministry of Encouragement," *Presbyterion* 11.1 (Spring 1985): 51–52. This entire article is worth a slow and thoughtful read.

5. *The Complete Works of Francis A. Schaeffer* (Wheaton: Crossway, 1982), 3:175–76; Jerram Barrs, "Francis Schaeffer: The Man and His Message," Covenant Seminary, October 24, 2012, http://www .covenantseminary.edu/the-thistle/francis-schaeffer-the-man-and-his-message; Bryan A. Follis, *Truth with Love: The Apologetics of Francis Schaeffer* (Wheaton: Crossway, 2006), 13.

REASONS WE'RE ON THE INJURED LIST

1) Prolonged Exhaustion

Prolonged exhaustion can be driven by the expectations of others in the church and also by our own prideful motivations.[6] Others may expect you to be present at every committee meeting to make decisions, every hospital room to pray, every church event to participate, and in everyone's living room for conversation and dessert. Sometimes, though, this can be driven by our desire for approval and our fear of disappointing others, and we *think* they have these expectations, even though they've never said that they do. Sometimes exhaustion comes from exceptionally fruitful seasons where the Spirit is at work in amazing and new ways. Whatever the reasons, prolonged exhaustion can cause significant physical and spiritual burnout, and it may seem that the only reasonable thing to do is to collapse (see Elijah's experience in 1 Kings 19).

2) Delight Turned to Duty

Delight can turn to duty in our own personal relationship with God and also in our calling to minister to others. There is an enormous temptation in ministry, because you are around the Word of God so often, to begin to treat it as something common and eventually unnecessary. Yes, you're preparing meals for others, but you haven't eaten from the feast yourself. Yes, you're fueling up others' tanks, but your own tank is running on empty. There can be an emotional deadness of soul that begins to make you wonder if God is really there. In our calling to minister to others, Martin Lloyd-Jones wisely points out two dangerous responses. First, we simply give up. The problems are too big. The difficulty has lasted too long. Delight has turned to duty, so we just quit. But Lloyd-Jones says there is a second response that is even more dangerous: resignation. The joy we once had is now gone, but we refuse to quit and will commit to keep on going, even though the passion is gone. "I will go on, though I go on feeling rather hopeless about it all, just shuffling down the road, not walking with hope as I once did, but keeping on as best I can."[7] Both of these dangers are very real when difficulty is overwhelming in the short run or exhausting in the long run.

6. See Tim Chester, *The Busy Christian's Guide to Busyness* (Nottingham: InterVarsity Press, 2006).

7. D. Martyn Lloyd-Jones, *Spiritual Depression: Its Causes and Its Cure* (Grand Rapids: Eerdmans, 1988), 194.

pre-concieved result

3 Mild Discouragement to Severe Depression

Most leaders have great expectations of how God is going to work in and through them and how God is going to transform the community of which they are a part. More often than not, our expectations are not met to the extent or in the timeframe we hope for. Nobody likes to be an Eeyore, but sometimes the sheep we minister to could accurately call us that if they were to see how our hearts respond to things not going the way we think they should. In ministry, there will be a thousand things that may cause mild discouragement to severe depression, and when we lose hope that God will work, it is easier to walk away from the situation.[8]

4 An Older-Brother View of Ministry

One of my twins was born with a life-threatening heart complication. Seven days after he was born, I found myself going one hundred miles an hour to get to the hospital to which he was being flown for immediate surgery. While the surgeons were preparing for surgery on my son, God was doing surgery on my heart. Like the older brother in the story of the prodigal son in Luke 15, I slowly began to realize that I felt entitled to life on easy street because I thought I had worked so hard and gone through so much in ministry. A horrible thought came through my mind: "God, I've been through so much and done so much for you, and this is what I get?" Immediately I realized I needed surgery. I had begun to see ministry as slaving for the Father, just like the older brother did (Luke 15:28–30), and was upset when the Father did things I didn't like. An older-brother mentality will make leaving easy when the Father doesn't do what you expect him to do.

5 Anger

Closely connected to an older-brother view of ministry is anger. "The first sign you have an elder-brother spirit is that when your life doesn't go as you want, you aren't just sorrowful but deeply angry and bitter."[9] I know

---

8. See Charles Spurgeon, "The Preacher's Fainting Fits," in *Lectures to My Students* (Pasadena: Pilgrim Publications, 1990), 167–79; Richard Winter, *Roots of Sorrow: Reflections on Depression and Hope* (Eugene, OR: Wipf and Stock, 2000); Edward T. Welch, *Depression: A Stubborn Darkness: A Light for the Path* (Greensboro, NC: New Growth Press, 2004); John Piper, *When the Darkness Does Not Lift: Doing What We Can While We Wait for God—and Joy* (Wheaton: Crossway, 2006).

9. Tim Keller, *The Prodigal God: Recovering the Heart of the Christian Faith* (New York: Dutton, 2008), 49.

that if I am honest about myself, I'm probably a mass murderer in Jesus' eyes (see Matt. 5:21–22). I may have the energy to maintain an outward façade of caring for others, but inwardly my heart may be raging at other people or the situation I am in. They have kept me from getting what I want or have threatened to take away something I have, and so, in my heart, the only appropriate response is anger.[10] If you stay angry long enough, you may begin to think that others are not worthy of your ministry or that people are impossible, so you might as well give up.

Fear, Anxiety, and Worry

If our ministry experiences have involved a lot of interpersonal conflict or congregational chaos, we may begin to be controlled by fear. If someone asks to come and talk to us, we know for sure that it's because he or she is either angry at us for doing something or disappointed in us for not doing something. We fear being exposed, humiliated, or rejected, and so we may stop visiting people, encouraging or correcting others, or making necessary phone calls. If we are going through a relatively peaceful season, we fear how soon the next conflict will develop. Our imaginations run wild with what could and probably will happen to us. Winston Churchill knew the negative power of fear to keep us from being faithful to our task: "You cannot tell from appearances how things will go. Sometimes imagination makes things out far worse than they are. . . . Those people who are imaginative see many more dangers than perhaps exist."[11] Because fear maximizes the problems, while minimizing the presence and power of God, faith is overpowered and almost crushed.[12]

Sinful Self-Indulgence

Our hearts restlessly seek anyone or anything in which to find satisfaction and joy. In marital counseling, I have found that couples who

---

10. See Dan Allender and Tremper Longman, *Bold Love* (Colorado Springs: NavPress, 1996), 257–60; Allender and Longman, *The Cry of the Soul: How Our Emotions Reveal Our Deepest Questions about God* (Colorado Springs: NavPress, 1994), 55–63.

11. Quoted by Steve Israel in *Charge! History's Greatest Military Speeches* (Annapolis: Naval Institute Press, 2007), 176.

12. See Guinness, *God in the Dark*; Edward T. Welch, *Running Scared: Fear, Worry, and the God of Rest* (Greensboro, NC: New Growth Press, 2007); Welch, *When People Are Big and God Is Small: Overcoming Peer Pressure, Codependency, and the Fear of Man* (Phillipsburg, NJ: P&R Publishing, 1997).

don't find their joy in Christ try to find their joy in each other. However, when the other person becomes a poor source of personal joy, one or both spouses begin to look for joy in either porn or an illegitimate relationship, or anything else that might provide what they are looking for. I think leaders can do the same thing in ministry. We are unaware that we are not rooting our ultimate and deepest joy in Christ, so we try to find joy in the midst of ministry, and if we don't find it there, we look for it somewhere else. Lloyd-Jones says that it is at these times that sin can become particularly appealing and ultimately enslaving.[13] This will have an enormous impact on our faith, our outlook on life, and our ministry, because "the principle of sin leads to the perspective of sin."[14]

This short list is by no means exhaustive, but it is intended to be a starting point for self-examination. All these things, over extended periods of time, can be reasons that our hearts begin to lose sight of the gospel and lack the strength that can only come from grace-empowered, prayerful dependence and patient persistence. Is there an older, wiser counselor who could speak deeply to our hearts?

SITTING DOWN WITH JOHN NEWTON

It would be wise to visit a counselor and listen to him carefully and reflectively before we make any decisions about our longevity in ministry. John Newton was a counselor to many, not only to those in his local church through his preaching, but also to the multitudes to whom he wrote letters. Newton sought to encourage and instruct a particular young minister who was, at times, overwhelmed by the difficulties of ministry. The comments below are culled from years of correspondence between the two pastors.

To begin with, Newton regularly counseled others not to listen to themselves or to unbelief in the middle of difficulty. He warned against listening to the continual voice of our own senses, our own hearts, or our own unbelief when we are tired or discouraged. That internal voice is incredibly insufficient and partial to fear and unbelief, and therefore we should not listen to its counsel.[15] Because our internal voice is not an

13. Lloyd-Jones, *Spiritual Depression*, 14.

14. Guinness, *God in the Dark*, 73.

15. *Wise Counsel: John Newton's Letters to John Ryland, Jr.*, ed. Grant Gordon (Carlisle, PA: Banner of Truth Trust, 2007), 189.

impartial witness, it seeks to undermine our faith and make us lose sight of the character, promises, and power of God in the midst of all the difficulty we are walking through. We often listen to ourselves and trust our own interpretation of things in the midst of difficulty, and also listen as we prophetically announce exactly what we think will happen in the near and distant future. Usually, it is only more pain.

Newton also counseled that difficulties and disappointments in ministry keep us from accomplishing what we want and make us discouraged by not allowing us to gain applause from others. Listen to Newton as he confesses his pride to a young pastor: "That Mr Self I have been speaking of would be glad to have a fine story to tell, of his importance and usefulness, how the people hang upon his words, and what wonders are done by it. He would like to send you a long list of conversions, that you might thence infer he is a very clever fellow."[16] How often do we feel ashamed of ourselves or envious of others when we speak with other leaders in ministry, because our situation isn't as exciting as we would like it to be? Mr. Self loves the applause of others and sinks when there is seemingly nothing thrilling to share.

As we continue to listen to Newton's counsel, we hear him give the much-needed caution that troubles in ministry can make us lose sight of God's sovereign faithfulness and often lead us into forgetfulness. God may have given us ninety-six or ninety-seven things out of a hundred, yet we are filled with impatience, frustration, and discouragement because we don't receive everything we want at once. When this happens, we lose sight of the other things God has given and therefore fail to live in joyful gratitude.[17] "We are selfish, ungrateful creatures; and if the Lord crosses or tries us in one thing, we are prone to forget our many calls for thankfulness. . . . We are liable to toss, like a wild bull in a net, or to sink into despondency."[18] With the loss of gratitude will come the loss of joy, which will lead to the loss of endurance. I have found Newton's comments to be hard to hear, but sorrowfully true of my own heart more than I'd like to admit.

We can also fail when we let difficulties overwhelm our minds and when we seek to control them on our own. How many nights have leaders lost

16. Ibid., 70.
17. Ibid., 124–25.
18. Ibid., 231–32.

sleep with anxiety? How often have leaders exhausted themselves in trying to fix a problem apart from prayerful dependence and patient faithfulness in everyday matters? Newton counsels against trying to plan exhaustively and think things out in our minds, which tends to lead us toward striving in our own strength to manipulate things to get what we want. A better path would be to patiently and prayerfully wait upon the will and timing of our gracious heavenly Father.[19] Newton learned this from his own experience, claiming to have often "hurt his own fingers" trying to "make crooked things straight" on his own, without the Lord's help and timing.[20] Can you sympathize with what Newton is saying?

Perhaps Newton's most emphatic insight is that we can so indulge grief and sorrow over difficulties that we lose sight of Calvary and eternity. In Psalms 42 and 43, the psalmist preaches to himself and refuses to drown in sorrow without speaking words of hope to his own heart. When their grief and sorrow last long enough, leaders can lose the energy needed to fight the fight of faith in their hearts. Although we may know that extended grief and prolonged discouragement can greatly disquiet our souls and exhaust our minds and bodies, "we are apt to indulge it, and to brood over sorrow till it gives a tincture to the whole frame of our spirits, and, perhaps, makes a lodgment in us, too deep to be removed. . . . Dally no more with grief; try to cut short all recollections that feed the anguish of the mind."[21] Overindulging in grief can minimize the effectiveness and longevity of our leadership. Leaders can rehearse their hurts and remind themselves constantly of their disappointments, but without also looking to the cross, these things can drown our hope and make us lose sight of the gospel.

ENTERING THE DANGER ZONE

If we fail to heed Scripture's counsel and Newton's counsel, we may very well experience a downward spiral where doubt begins to be the only thing of which we are certain. We can become so overwhelmed by circumstantial and relational difficulties within ministry that we forget the incredible news of what we once were and what God's grace has made us. Once we forget the good news, it won't be long before we become overwhelmed

19. Ibid., 154.
20. Ibid., 223.
21. Ibid., 193.

with doubt when we feel the disappointment coming again. So the danger zone in ministry begins with forgetfulness and a loss of amazement and awe at what God has done for us.[22]

The danger zone also includes a loss of identity. There has been a functional forgetting that we are the treasured possession, the fully adopted and forever-loved children of the living God. Our identity drifts away from being in Christ and drifts toward being located in our function as a leader. It is tempting to see our worth and value in what we do and are able to accomplish, rather than in the free grace of God's love. If we begin to see ourselves merely as hirelings, rather than as heralds chosen and called by God, we'll walk away when the going gets tough.

Perhaps the center of the danger zone is the loss of spiritual vitality and hope. We may feel crushed, exhausted, and spiritually empty. God doesn't seem to answer our prayers. Time in the Word, if spent at all, is not refreshing, but rather dull and monotonous. Every day seems to be filled with the same things. Prayers for renewal for the leader and the church have been prayed, but nothing seems to change. There has been diligent ministry, but there seems to be no real, lasting, and substantial fruit in anyone's life to show for it. Despite faithfully preaching and ministering the gospel, there are still marriages falling apart, addictions that are enslaving, bitter groups within the congregation, people leaving to go to other churches, and so on. Hope begins to fade, and when hope fades, so does the ability to endure patiently and joyfully.

Os Guinness has noted that faith must be put into practice or it will become useless. Faith does not automatically respond when the difficulty hits or lingers, but must actively be put to use in how one thinks about or responds to the situation. When this doesn't happen, faith "is not eaten away suddenly, but nibbled at the corners. It is not hit by a bolt of lightning, it is the victim of the slow erosion of many winters." Oftentimes there can be a subtle, almost unconscious drifting away from the faith.[23]

---

22. Guinness, *God in the Dark*, 39–56; Paul David Tripp, *Dangerous Calling: Confronting the Unique Challenges of Pastoral Ministry* (Wheaton: Crossway, 2012), 113–24.

23. Guinness, *God in the Dark*, 118–19. He goes on to quote C. S. Lewis: "I think the trouble with me is *lack of faith*. I have no *rational* ground for going back on the arguments that convinced me of God's existence: but the irrational deadweight of my old sceptical habits, and the spirit of this age, and the cares of the day, steal away all my lively feeling of the truth, and often when I pray I wonder if I am not posting letters to a nonexistent address. Mind you I don't *think* so—the whole of my reasonable mind is convinced: but I often *feel* so."

need sabbatical

e.g   I was in that danger zone at one point in my own ministry. I met with an elder, as I've already shared, and told him to pray that God would show up or he'd have my resignation in a few days. I was willing to be a statistic of pastors leaving the ministry, if it meant me keeping my sanity and perhaps my faith. What I didn't share with him, or with my wife, was that my faith seemed to be almost gone.[24] I was rocked to the core, not knowing what to think about life, ministry, and Christianity. I desperately wanted God to show up, but sincerely disbelieved that he would. As I drove into the mountains, alone, I wondered, "What will I do if I conclude this isn't true?" My only thought was what Paul says in 1 Corinthians 15:32: if the resurrection isn't true, "let us eat and drink, for tomorrow we die."

QUESTIONS FOR REFLECTION

1. In the list of things mentioned in this chapter that can lead to doubt, which one do you struggle with the most? Is there anyone in your life that you can share that with, so that he or she can encourage you and pray for you about it?

2. Which aspect of John Newton's counsel convicted or comforted you the most? Why?

3. Medical forms have an "in case of emergency call" section that tell people whom to contact in case of a physical emergency. Do you have someone you can confide in if you are going through a spiritual emergency? Do you need to contact that person right now?

24. While I *felt* this way, I passionately affirm that we cannot lose our faith or salvation, because our salvation rests in the object of our faith and not in the strength of our faith. When we are faithless—he remains faithful, for he cannot deny himself (2 Tim. 2:13).

TRANSITION

THE REMEDY OF THE CROSS

"We must never forget that the place where the triumph of evil seemed so obvious and God's saving care seemed most hidden was at the cross. God's sovereign rule over nature and history in general cannot be separated from his saving purpose. Just as we find God in the 'low places' of this world—lying in a dirty feeding trough in Bethlehem, wearily treading the road to Jerusalem, and crying out in dereliction on the cross—we trust that he is most present in our lives precisely where he seems most hidden." —Michael Horton[1]

Gordon Mathewson

issues re-cap

JOHN CALVIN has a chapter in his *Institutes* that should be read on a regular basis by any and all in church leadership. Chapter 8 of book 3 is entitled "Bearing the Cross, A Part of Self-Denial." In the previous chapters of this book, I have sought to focus on the external difficulties of ministry, the inward idolatries that often drive ministry, the functional (rather than professed) theology that can often inform and impel ministry, and finally the overwhelmed heart that often leaves ministry. In dealing with these matters, genuinely "bearing the cross" is something that, if we are honest, we often want to avoid doing. To use Kevin Vanhoozer's terminology, becoming angry, bitter, distant, and cold, and potentially leaving

---

1. Michael Horton, *The Christian Faith: A Systematic Theology for Pilgrims on the Way* (Grand Rapids: Zondervan, 2011), 363.

or simply not engaging in the ministry to which we've been called, is not "fitting participation" in light of the drama of redemption.

Calvin wisely addresses this issue by calling on all believers—and specifically leaders in the church—to deny themselves and take up their cross. To any and all who seek to grow in Christ and help others mature in Christ, the Father graciously gives "what is healthful for each man," namely, "the remedy of the cross."[2] Only by dying to self, through the means provided at Calvary, can any leader be healed of the undercurrent of selfishness in his heart.

Many, early in their ministry, expect incredible "blessings" (often defined by their own idolatrous desires, not by the Word of God), but Calvin calls each of us to prepare for a life filled with various difficulties and frequent disappointments.[3] It is precisely because we have been adopted by the Father in Christ that we can expect to share Christ's sufferings in this life and share in his glory only in the life hereafter. Ironically, as we saw in the last chapter, the very sufferings that cause us to doubt our calling, or even our faith, are the same sufferings through which God wants to confirm our faith in, and fellowship with, Christ![4]

Yet, these sufferings come with a wise purpose. As we pass through our lives, which are a "continual cross," we are taught to trust more in the faithfulness of God than in our own strength, wisdom, and virtue. The more we are humbled, the more we learn to call upon his power and come to a deeper knowledge of our Father.[5] Only the cross can get to the root of our dependence upon our own strength and wisdom.[6] Through the crosses that we bear, we learn to patiently endure by the power of God—"an endurance quite unattainable by their own effort."[7] As we experience these trials, we also experience the power of Christ's resurrection.[8]

As you read slowly and reflectively through this section, you may get the feeling that Calvin is saying, "C'mon, man. Life is going to be hard. Ministry is going to be difficult. God said it would. Trust God. Be happy.

---

2. John Calvin, *Institutes of the Christian Religion*, ed. John T. McNeill, trans. Ford Lewis Battles, 2 vols., The Library of Christian Classics (Philadelphia: Westminster Press, 1960), 3.8.5.

3. Ibid., 3.8.1.

4. Ibid.

5. Ibid., 3.8.2.

6. Ibid., 3.8.3.

7. Ibid.

8. Ibid., 3.8.1.

Eat a Snickers and keep going." However, Calvin doesn't say that. He readily admits that the joy that should come from knowing Christ and being saved by him, trusting in his good purposes in the midst of trials, doesn't require a cheerfulness of us "as to remove all feeling of bitterness and pain."[9] If we went through everything with nothing but cheerfulness, there would be no need for patient endurance. The Christian is able to give expression to his pain and sorrow, and is encouraged to do so, because this is precisely what the Savior did: "For he groaned and wept both over his own and others' misfortunes. And he taught his disciples to do the same."[10] Yet, at the same time, there remains a deeper joy that comes from communion with God and empowers endurance: "For Scripture praises the saints for their forbearance when, so afflicted with harsh misfortune, they do not break or fall; so stabbed with bitterness, they are at the same time flooded with spiritual joy; so pressed by apprehension, they recover their breath, revived by God's consolation."[11] It is necessary and essential for patient endurance in ministry, that the "bitterness of the cross be tempered with spiritual joy."[12]

Thus, Calvin reminds us of our call to take up our cross and follow Christ (Matt. 16:24). We follow Christ to the death of our sinful heart and our selfish dreams and awake in resurrection power to the motivation of God's glory and the desire for his kingdom to come and not our own.

In the next section of this book, I want to take you on a journey to learn what a more fitting response may look like in light of the drama of redemption that began with a promise, climaxed on a cross, and ended with conquering death and reigning at the right hand of the Father. We'll seek to understand the thrill of resurrection power, the call to suffering servanthood, the need to fight for unity, and God's desire for us to be in ministry for the long haul.

Let's pick up our crosses and get going.

9. Ibid., 3.8.8.
10. Ibid., 3.8.9.
11. Ibid., 3.8.10.
12. Ibid., 3.8.11.

6

RESURRECTED TO LIFE AND HOPE

CHRISTIANITY MAKES truth claims about events that happened in history and took place in public, where individuals either did or did not experience what the authors of the Bible say they did. When I first came to faith in Christ, I simply accepted the testimony of the Bible as to what happened. Yet there are times and reasons that may occasion the question: "Is this really true? Did it really happen? Was Jesus really raised from the dead? Was the Spirit really poured out in power? Is this really worth it?" That's precisely where I was as I drove into the little mountain town of Cherokee, North Carolina. Either Jesus really did conquer death and is reigning at the right hand of the Father, or he didn't—and I needed to choose a vocation that required less "skin in the game" and try to have a nice life before death ruined it all forever.

I had experienced so much weakness in myself and had seen so much weakness within the walls of the church that I was fairly convinced that there was no way that Jesus was powerfully reigning from the throne. However, I knew that if Jesus was alive and reigning, it would change everything about how I viewed ministry and how I would enter back into it.

I decided to investigate. *"=ck-it-out"

BELIEVING IN THE RESURRECTION—AGAIN

Along with my Bible, I took a small box of books with me and sat next to a small stream in the middle of the Smoky Mountains.[1] I prayed

1. They were: Richard Bauckham, *Jesus and the Eyewitnesses: The Gospels as Eyewitness Testimony* (Grand Rapids: Eerdmans, 2006); C. A. J. Coady, *Testimony: A Philosophical Study* (Oxford: Oxford University Press, 1995); Craig Blomberg, *The Historical Reliability of the Gospels* (Downers Grove,

desperate prayers for help and insight, and when I couldn't or didn't want to pray anymore, I took a measure of comfort in the biblical claim that if all this was really true, the Spirit was interceding within me and for me with groans too deep for words (Rom. 8:26).

Slowly but surely, God began to breathe life back into me as I read. I began to see that I was like Thomas, demanding exhaustive proof rather than sufficient evidence. Thomas should've taken his friends at their word, but he didn't. I was in that boat too. I know the New Testament claims that Jesus rose, but does it really make sense? Grateful for God's mercy, I came away more convinced than ever. Here's why.

What struck me initially was the transparency of the biblical claims. The disciples should have *easily* believed, but they were the first to *greatly* doubt the resurrection—and the New Testament doesn't even try to cover this up. It was just as hard for them to believe it then as it is for us now. Women were the first eyewitnesses of the resurrection, and their testimony wouldn't have even have been allowed in court at that time. There are seeming discrepancies among the gospel accounts of the details surrounding what happened.[2] If the resurrection was a myth and the disciples had been seeking merely to gain religious power, they would have smoothed out and corrected these difficulties. Scripture also claims that over five hundred people saw the resurrected Jesus, and that anyone who was curious could go have a conversation with them.[3]

Another major factor in coming back to the core conviction of the resurrection was the radical and immediate shift in worldviews and religious practices that followed. In the Greco-Roman culture, the idea of resurrection was considered both impossible and undesirable. Nobody had ever seen a resurrection occur, and for them the concept of physicality after death was bad news, not good news. In the Jewish culture, the notion of an individual

---

IL: InterVarsity Press, 1987); Tim Keller, *The Reason for God: Belief in an Age of Skepticism* (New York: Dutton, 2008); N. T. Wright, *The Resurrection of the Son of God* (Minneapolis: Fortress Press, 2003); Michael Horton, *We Believe: Recovering the Essentials of the Apostles Creed* (Nashville: Word Publishing, 1998); Mark Driscoll and Gerry Breshears, *Vintage Jesus: Timeless Answers to Timely Questions* (Wheaton: Crossway, 2007); William Lane Craig, *The Son Rises: Historical Evidences for the Resurrection of Jesus* (Eugene, OR: Wipf and Stock, 2000).

2. Most scholars point out that multiple eyewitness accounts that are perfectly in line with each other are the ones that we are to be skeptical of, whereas minor differences tend to convey the reality of what actually occurred.

3. That is exactly what Luke did as he sought to present to Theophilus a careful, well-researched, orderly account of everything that had happened in those days. See Luke 1:1–4.

being raised from the dead prior to the judgment day was unthinkable . . . inconceivable. Yet both Jews and Gentiles were placing their faith in a resurrected Messiah overnight. Furthermore, Jewish believers also changed some of their most highly cherished and traditionally sacred practices (e.g., moving worship from Saturday to Sunday; worshipping Christ as God), the breaking of which had often led to stoning in the past.[4]

The explosive and expansive growth of the early church is also an important reality to bring into consideration. Prior to their witnessing of the risen Christ, the disciples were fearful, timid, and cowardly. They had failed, they had fled, and they were afraid. However, practically overnight again, they became fearless of death and passionate in their proclamation of a risen Savior. If the disciples had stolen the body and knew the resurrection was a lie, would they have so winsomely communicated this lie and passionately given their lives for this falsehood? The overnight change of the disciples from cowardly to courageous and the immediate and expansive growth of the church are best explained if the disciples had encountered a risen Savior.

So why is this important for ministry? It means that human guilt has been dealt with finally and fully. It means that death has not only been confronted, but conquered. It means that new and true life can be experienced before death, and eternal life after death. It means that hope for better things has gone from the category of "maybe" to a definite certainty. It means that a new heavens and a new earth, where those who trust in Christ will live forever, is coming. It means that God is already beginning the process of making all things new, as the age to come is breaking into this present evil age. It means that God gives resurrection power, so that leaders can endure.

I woke up in my hotel room on the final morning and went to the same rock in the middle of the same little creek, and my heart was no longer filled with doubt, fear, and questions, but worship. Jesus had risen from the grave. Jesus was causing the sun to shine, the breeze to blow, the water to trickle, my heart to be filled, his people to grow, and others to come to know him. I was eager to talk to the elder and tell him that, whatever

---

4. This is incredibly important because, as Thomas Kuhn points out, major worldviews (which, for our purposes, include religious practice) often take years or decades to change, during a slow and very complex process. See Thomas Kuhn, *The Structure of Scientific Revolutions*, 3rd ed. (Chicago: University of Chicago Press, 1996).

he had been praying, God had answered his prayers for me. The Great
Shepherd had taken a wandering and injured sheep and brought him back,
bound him up, and placed him beside still waters (literally and spiritually!).

EXPERIENCING RESURRECTION . . . AGAIN

The resurrection has profound implications for ministry. It means the
resurrection of hardened hearts, the resurrection of our hope, the resurrection of our joy, and the resurrection of our endurance.

The Resurrection of Our Hearts

If God can raise Jesus from the dead, he is powerful enough to pour
life back into a hardened and cold heart. One of my favorite promises
in the entire Bible comes from Psalm 34:18, "The LORD is near to the
brokenhearted and saves the crushed in spirit." They are either crushed
by life's circumstances or by their own sin, and I am often crushed by
both. Yet this doesn't disqualify us from God's presence, but actually
makes Him eager and willing to serve us by renewing and reviving us
(Isa. 57:15). Incredibly, this God, who is rich in mercy and loves us with
a great love (Eph. 2:4), uses the "immeasurable greatness" of his resurrection power (Eph. 1:19) to strengthen our hearts (Eph. 3:16) and fill
us with his fullness (Eph. 3:19).

The resurrection, then, is good news for pastors who are exhausted
and crushed by life, ministry, and their own sins. It means the resurrected
Shepherd of the sheep will find you to strengthen you once again with his
resurrection power (Isa. 40:11, 27–31). The King of life will breathe life into
you once again by the Spirit and grant you new repentance, strengthened
faith, and a refreshed heart. It is the repentant heart that has the most room
for the rivers of living water flowing from the heart of our King.[5]

The Resurrection of Our Hope

If God can raise Jesus from the dead, He is powerful enough to keep
my faith and hope in his promises and purposes alive. "Hope deferred
makes the heart sick" (Prov. 13:12). It took me way too long in ministry

5. See C. John Miller, *Repentance and 21st Century Man* (Fort Washington, PA: CLC Publishing, 2003), 54.

to realize that I was hoping for promises to be fulfilled that God had not made. I was hoping for incredible kingdom impact (which, for most pastors, usually translates into fast and sizeable church growth). I was hoping for the joy of being used greatly in the kingdom (which, in my mind, usually translates into being widely respected by others). When that didn't happen, I felt sick—because my hope was in the wrong places. Even when my motivations and expectations were more in line with God's, I found myself echoing the heart of the suffering servant, "But I said, 'I have labored in vain; I have spent my strength for nothing and vanity'" (Isa. 49:4a). Yet the Servant didn't respond in cynical unbelief, as I often can. While this was his first thought, it definitely wasn't his last.

His next words are, "Yet surely my right is with the LORD, and my recompense with my God" (49:4). "To the Servant all seems a waste of effort, but he turns from his own wisdom and rests in the God who called and appointed him. . . . He sees nothing coming out of all his effort, but it is not for him to decide. . . . He has been faithful . . . now it is for the Lord to bring what fruit he will out of it all."[6] In other words, the Servant hoped in God's power, wisdom, and purposes. The resurrection, then, is good news for pastors because it means that the resurrected Shepherd of the sheep will restore your hope in the promises he *has made* and the purposes he *will accomplish*. He *will* bring to perfection that which he began, and he will do it in his way and in his time, but he will do it and will give you resurrected hope for it.[7]

The Resurrection of Our Joy

If God can raise Jesus from the dead, he is powerful enough to keep my joy focused on and rooted in the completed work of Jesus Christ. My wife and I went on a date, and she made a little joke that made us both laugh hysterically—and then cry. We realized we hadn't laughed like that in over a year in the midst of difficult ministry circumstances. I had lost sight of the joy we have in Christ and the joy that is supposed to characterize the kingdom. I had made my joy contingent on good circumstances and faithful

6. J. Alec Motyer, *The Prophecy of Isaiah: An Introduction and Commentary* (Downers Grove, IL: InterVarsity Press, 1993), 387.

7. See Paul David Tripp, *Forever: Why You Can't Live without It* (Grand Rapids: Zondervan, 2007), 92–106.

people. The ups and downs of my heart and attitude took a tremendous toll on my wife and kids. I was rooting my joy in all the wrong things.

There are things in life and in ministry that do and should cause sorrow, but Paul says there can be a deeper joy that cannot be touched by the circumstances of life (2 Cor. 6:10). This joy is rooted in the work of a Savior who loved us, gave himself for us, and reigns in heaven on our behalf. This joy is also rooted in our confidence that all God's promises are yes and amen in Christ (Rom. 12:12; 2 Cor. 1:20). If you are crushed and exhausted and joyless, the resurrected Shepherd will restore your joy in being forgiven (Ps. 51:10), being adopted (Gal. 4:5), and having your name written in heaven (Luke 10:20). I love how C. S. Lewis describes the joy in Narnia when everyone danced with Aslan after he defeated the White Witch:

> It was such a romp as no one has ever had except in Narnia; and whether it was more like playing with a thunderstorm or playing with a kitten Lucy could never make up her mind.[8]

The God who is "high and lifted up, who inhabits eternity, whose name is Holy" and is "a consuming fire," is the same God who was born in a cattle trough, died on a cross, defeated death, and rose from the grave to dwell with his people (Isa. 57:15; Deut. 4:24; John 14:23). This reality of God's incredible holiness, blended with his condescending love in the gospel, is the crucial foundation for the joy that is to be our strength as we serve others (Neh. 8:10).

The Resurrection of Our Endurance

If God can raise Jesus from the dead, he is powerful enough to empower my endurance as I work tirelessly for the joy of others. Paul says that he ministered to others, not for his own comfort, but for their "progress and joy in the faith" (Phil. 1:25–26). Amid all the joys and sorrows, difficulties and delights, God calls us to faithfully endure in ministry to others for their "progress and joy in the faith." Knowing the resurrection power available to believers, Paul prayed that believers would "be strengthened with all power, according to his glorious might, for all endurance and patience

8. C. S. Lewis, *The Chronicles of Narnia* (New York: Harper Collins, 2007), 185.

with joy" (Col. 1:11). "Endurance is a purposeful 'abiding under' what is hard and painful, considering others even when you don't feel good," and the only way this happens is through resurrection power.[9] In the midst of ministry, it is the strength of our resurrected Savior that so "powerfully works within" us (Col. 1:29).

This is good news for ministry leaders because it means that our resurrected King will definitely give strength to the crushed, exhausted, and almost quitting, so that when we run we will not be weary, and when we walk we will not faint (Isa. 40:27–31). It was the joy set before Christ that strengthened him to endure the cross (Heb. 12:2), and it is the joy of the gospel and the certain hope of eternity with Christ in the new heavens and new earth that strengthen us to endure the ups and downs, the joys and sorrows, and the difficulties and delights of ministry.

THE POWER OF THE RESURRECTION MANIFESTED IN WEAKNESS AND DEATH

All this talk about resurrection and resurrection power raises the question of what the kingdom of God looks like when it comes in our hearts and in our communities. Are we to expect spiritual fireworks, mystical experiences, mass conversions, cultural transformation, and expansive kingdom growth in a short period of time and in an ever-repeating cycle? A theology of glory would say "absolutely!" while a theology of the cross would say "not exactly."

D. A. Carson wisely cautions ministry leaders when he says that we cannot mistake D-Day for V-Day.[10] While the deathblow has been dealt, the full and final victory is yet to come. The fundamental character of our existence is "suffering with Christ," and Christ's ascension power is manifested in the *suffering* church.[11] Does this "suffering" consist only of persecution? No. It also includes "the mundane, 'trivial' but often so easily

9. David Powlison, "God's Grace and Your Suffering," in *Suffering and the Sovereignty of God*, ed. John Piper and Justin Taylor (Wheaton: Crossway, 2006), 165.

10. D. A. Carson, *A Model of Christian Maturity: An Exposition of 2 Corinthians 10–13* (Grand Rapids: Baker, 2007), 54.

11. Richard B. Gaffin, Jr., "Theonomy and Eschatology," in *Theonomy: A Reformed Critique*, ed. William S. Barker and W. Robert Godfrey (Grand Rapids: Zondervan, 1990), 211–12. See also Richard B. Gaffin, Jr., "The Usefulness of the Cross," *Westminster Theological Journal* 41 (1979): 228–46. I am grateful to my professor, Dr. Bryan Estelle, for encouraging a thoughtful, careful, and reflective reading of these articles for their impact on our pastoral ministry.

exasperating and unsettling frustrations of daily living."[12] It is right there, in the midst of those "exasperating and unsettling frustrations of daily living," where we experience, but do not always feel completely, Christ's resurrection power. Where do we find this power? We find it whenever we fellowship with Christ in his sufferings, being conformed to his death, and feel profound weakness. "Theirs is a fellowship in which his power is made perfect, not alongside of or beyond, but *in* their weakness (2 Cor. 12:9, 10). His limitless power is manifested through the medium of their pervasive and extreme weakness."[13]

It is precisely those times when I feel most weak, most hurt, most foolish, and most exhausted that I most want to give in. Yet, it is precisely in those same moments that God's power can be perfected in our weakness (2 Cor. 12:9), and he can strengthen us to keep going and remain faithful to the call to ministry.[14]

Resurrection power is within us and all around us, and it takes the work of the Spirit to help us see it. When my heart was enraptured by a functional theology of glory, I expected incredible and visible results to occur on a regular basis, but I completely missed so many areas in which resurrection power was at work. A theology of the cross helped me see resurrection power when I would look out on Sunday morning and see a teenager broken, but still worshipping, even though his dad had died of cancer a few nights before. Resurrection power is evident when a father gives the eulogy at the funeral of his daughter who died after seven months in utero and explains how she is dressed in white in the tiny coffin, but is now with her true husband, Jesus Christ, even though he longed as a father to give her away in the future to a godly young man.

Resurrection power is at work when a young couple realizes they won't be able to have children of their own, but, knowing that God is good, still seek him in prayer, are transparent with others about their pain, and share how the Bible is giving them comfort. Resurrection power is at work when a ninety-seven-year-old widow, who held the hand of her husband every day until he died, welcomes the pastor into her house at 2 a.m. with the rest of the family and says, "Every time I looked into his eyes, I saw

12. Gaffin, "Theonomy and Eschatology," 214.
13. Gaffin, "The Usefulness of the Cross," 240.
14. See J. I. Packer, *Weakness Is the Way: Life with Christ Our Strength* (Wheaton: Crossway, 2013).

Jesus." This power is at work when deacons serve meals to the poor in the neighborhood in the name of Christ.

I counseled a young couple who were getting a divorce without biblical warrant. I met with them individually and as a couple, but both were committed to going down the path they had chosen. I asked them, "Do you believe in the resurrection?" "Of course," they said. I gently responded, "So you believe God can raise Jesus from the dead and give you new spiritual life, but that he doesn't have the power to resurrect and transform your marriage?" Let's just say there was enough anger at that comment to make them leave my office. I later left a voicemail on their phone: "Please, please don't do this. Imagine God's power enabling you to love each other when it's hard, to serve each other when you don't feel like it. Imagine being so madly in love that you take your children to a park, set up a picnic, play your favorite song, and dance in front of your children." I never got a call back. But one of them walked into my office a year and a half later in tears. I was sure that I was about to hear that the divorce had been finalized. But I was told: "We had a picnic and danced in front of our children. It's been _PTL_ amazing what God has done."

God met them in their weakness and made them strong. Resurrection power meets us and empowers us when we acknowledge and experience the absolute depths of our weakness, frailty, and failures. Resurrection power may heal the hurt, or it may simply give us the strength to endure. Either way, resurrection power meets us in our weakness.

Let me say this. Jesus alone is the husband of his bride, the church. Yet are there times when you want to leave? Are there times when she has said so many hard things and done so many difficult things that you're thinking of walking in the other direction? Have you seen too many blemishes on her dress and spots on her character? Let me ask this, as I've had to ask myself on a regular basis: Do you believe in the resurrection? Do you believe that God is powerful enough to meet you and meet her in the midst of the hardships, in the midst of the pain, in the midst of the struggle, the suffering, and the sinning?

_Pp 240_ Jesus today has many who love his heavenly kingdom, but few who carry his cross; many who yearn for comfort, few who long for distress. Plenty of people he finds to share his banquet, few to share his fast. Everyone desires to take part in his rejoicing, but few are willing to suffer anything

85

> for his sake. There are many that follow Jesus as far as the breaking of bread, few as far as drinking the cup of suffering; many that revere his miracles, few that follow him in the indignity of the cross.[15]

In 1 Corinthians 15:4, Paul says that Christ "was raised on the third day in accordance with the Scriptures." This truth changes everything. This power is experienced as you share in Christ's sufferings and are conformed to his death (Phil. 3:10). His power is made perfect in *your* weakness. His power is made perfect in *their* weakness. It sustains you in the middle of suffering and helps you marvel at the simple.

He is risen! He is risen indeed!

Go on a picnic. Turn up the gospel music. Maybe you'll even dance.

QUESTIONS FOR REFLECTION

1. What are some practical implications of the resurrection in your own heart and life?
2. How does the resurrection give you hope for those around you?
3. If God were to open your eyes to see tangible ways in which resurrection power is subtly manifesting itself in the lives of those around you, what would you see happening?

---

15. Thomas à Kempis, quoted in Philip Graham Ryken, "Pastoral Ministry in Union with Christ," in *The Practical Calvinist: An Introduction to the Presbyterian and Reformed Heritage,* ed. Peter A. Lillback (Fearn, Ross-shire: Christian Focus Publishing, 2002), 453.

7
SOMEBODY LOVES YOU

THERE'S A WONDERFUL children's book named *Somebody Loves You, Mr. Hatch!* It tells the story of a man who wakes up every morning, buys a newspaper, but never says hello to the man working at the newsstand. He walks past children playing hopscotch right outside his door, without even a smile. He works silently at his job—at a shoe-lace factory. He has the same lunch every day—a cheese and mustard sandwich with a prune for dessert—and does not sit with anyone or speak to anyone. He goes home alone. He eats dinner alone and goes to bed alone—every day.

One day, however, Mr. Hatch gets a package from the mailman. It is a Valentine's Day box of candy with a card that says simply, "Somebody loves you." It changes his life significantly. He joyfully plays hopscotch with the children outside his door. Instead of just buying a paper, he speaks to the man at the newsstand. He bakes brownies for the neighbors. He is a changed man. He enjoys and serves others because someone loves him.

But all his joy and all his love for others come to a crashing halt when the mailman shows up once again, but this time to ask for the package. It was delivered to the wrong address! Mr. Hatch is devastated and returns to his normal routine, not showing much love to those around him. In his mind, nobody loves him.[1]

This remarkable children's story teaches a deep spiritual truth about loving and serving others: we will joyfully and sacrificially serve others when we know that we are loved by someone else. To the extent that we do not know that we are loved, we will not love others.

1. Eileen Spinelli, *Somebody Loves You, Mr. Hatch* (New York: Simon and Schuster, 1996).

THE FAILURE OF LOVE

One of the most remarkable things that Scripture reveals about the human heart is our tendency to forget. Israel forgot God's power, presence, and love continually. So do we. Sadly, even ministry leaders can go about their daily work the way Mr. Hatch worked at the shoelace factory—functioning and getting the job done, but their heart just isn't in it. We've forgotten that Somebody loves us.

Because I share so much in common with Mr. Hatch and often forget that I am justified and adopted by my loving heavenly Father, I might have been tempted to write the letter to the Philippians a little differently than Paul did:

> Troublemakers,
>
> I'm so sick and tired of how difficult you make my life. All I hear about from others who know you and all I experience from you is arguing, complaining, fighting, and rampant selfishness. Yes, I know you've helped me in my mission. I know you've given me a generous financial gift, and I know you do some other good things, but the thing that really gets under my skin is how little progress you've made in the faith and how close you are as a church and as individuals to imploding and destroying your witness for Christ. Stop it! Get your act together. Next time I come, I want to see that you've thrown out the troublemakers and have learned to get along. Euodia and Syntyche . . . seriously? Grow up.
>
> You're such a pain.
>
> Oh, I forgot to tell you, I love you and hope to see you soon.
>
> Your apostle,
>
> Paul

When we forget that somebody loves us, it is hard to love others the way Paul outlines in 1 Corinthians 13, and we may just write an e-mail or make a phone call similar to the letter you just read. That's why I want to spend more time on two specific aspects of love that Paul mentions in the great love chapter that I think are especially difficult for ministry leaders.

First, love is not irritable. "To be irritable is to be in a constant count-down for a temperamental blast-off. It is to have your insides coiled, ready to spring into fury. The spiritual membranes of an irritable person are inflamed; the slightest friction sends a surge of pain through his system."[2] In other words, the love inside of our hearts can be padlocked, whereas our anger often has a hair trigger. Irritability can be expressed through deep sighs, rolled eyes, a sharpened tone, gritted teeth, or prolonged discussions on how someone else messed everything up. The sources of irritability in ministry can be legion, but the core, often contrary to what we might think it may be, tends to be a heart that says, "I want, but I don't have" (see James 4:1–2).

Irritability can come from sinking our deepest joy into good circum-stances and cooperative people, and when these things are not delivered on the same day, we become angry. Irritability can come from losing a spiritual perspective that allows us to multiply reasons to be grateful even in the midst of difficulty. A heart that knows that somebody loves them finds ample reasons for thanksgiving and thus results in a joyful demeanor, knowing that God's love and grace are the ultimate source of our joy, not the people or circumstances that surround us. Yet once we lose this grati-tude and joy and become irritable, we begin to resemble Sesame Street's "Grouch" character more than we do our own Savior. Love is not irritable.

Second, love is not resentful. It does not keep a record of wrongs. It's very easy in ministry, especially when someone fails or hurts you, to keep a nice pad of paper in your mind with a list. Each time they hurt you or disappoint you, it becomes another item on your list. Eventually the list gets too large, and a situation arises that tempts you to get out your list and angrily fire off every single time they've disappointed or hurt you. Perhaps you do. Or perhaps you stay awake at night and hit "replay" in your mind to relive all the ways you've been hurt, even though you never speak with the individual or group. The pain and anger grow.

This resentment destroys our perception of others and diminishes our affection for them. "Resentment is doubly deadly because it views the real person, whose fault is being kept alive, through a lens fouled by anger."[3]

2. Lewis Smedes, *Love within Limits: A Realist's View of 1 Corinthians 13* (Grand Rapids: Eerd-mans, 1978), 56.
3. Ibid., 69.

Even though someone may have hurt us once or twice, we convince ourselves that that person is always hurtful toward everyone. The hurt they've caused us now becomes their identity in our eyes. We convince ourselves that we are justified in our anger toward them and in our avoidance of them. We've lost sight of their total character, unable to remember any good that they have ever done. It cools our affections and hardens our heart toward that person.[4] When we forget that Somebody loves us, if others fail in their love for us, irritability and resentment can become our best friends. We will no longer be able to bear all things, believe all things, hope all things, or endure all things (1 Cor. 13:7). Sadly, if we become irritable or resentful, we're often the last ones to notice, and we probably become angry if someone expresses concern about our being that way.

Counselor Ed Welch makes a further point about how resentment or anger can grow to include entire groups of people or even whole churches: the hurt individual can "generalize from the specific case to the entire church: If one person hurt me, then the church hurt me."[5] Oftentimes leaders can become completely blind to, first of all, their own significant contribution to the issue at hand, and, second of all, the various ways in which individuals in the church have genuinely loved and cared for them. Yet because one individual or a few more *may* have said or done something hurtful, the entire group or church is found guilty and sentenced to endure our coldness and resentment. The bride of Christ has become public enemy number one in our hearts.

In light of the above, if you need to grow in your ability to genuinely and deeply repent (and we all do!), just read 1 Corinthians 13:4–7 and put your name wherever the word *love* shows up, and think deeply about what love is and isn't. If it were me, I'd write, "Clay is patient and kind; Clay does not envy or boast; Clay is not arrogant or rude," and so forth. However, I'd be concerned that someone could accuse me of lying! I desperately long for these things to be true of me, and I hope that they are to some extent, but I fall short of these things on a daily basis.

For instance, when things get difficult because of difficult people, I know I can become a major pharisee and often be totally oblivious to that

4. Ibid., 71.

5. Edward T. Welch, *When People Are Big and God Is Small: Overcoming Peer Pressure, Codependency, and the Fear of Man* (Phillipsburg, NJ: P&R Publishing, 1997), 197.

fact. Externally, I may be striving to express loving words and actions, but internally I may be thinking, "I can't believe they just said that—they are so rude. I'm glad I'm not like that." Or, "How could anybody do that and be a leader? That was ridiculous, outrageous, and mind-boggling! They are so immature and childish. Glad I'm not like that." I can even become the anti-pharisee pharisee: "I'm sure glad that I'm not like one of those pharisees!" "Love is not arrogant," Paul writes. And yet, my proud heart boastfully claims to be better than someone else.

In contrast to the way we can sometimes respond to the difficulties of life and ministry, notice what Paul *actually* says to the Philippians. He calls them "saints," not troublemakers (1:1). Rather than grumbling, he joyfully prays with gratitude for each and every one of them, even those who are acting less than mature (1:4). He is confident that God will finish the work of grace in them that he began when they came to faith (1:6). But the most striking thing Paul says comes in verse 8: "For God is my witness, how I yearn for you all with the affection of Christ Jesus."

One of the first things to notice is Paul's seriousness and sincerity. He begins with an oath, "God is my witness." Paul is incredibly serious. He doesn't have his fingers crossed behind his back as he says something that he has to say simply because he is a pastor. Rather, he speaks with sincerity and truth. Next, deep within his heart he has an incredibly intense desire not to avoid them, but simply to be with them. And notice this: his intense desire is to be with every single one of them, "even those whose antics so often seem to bring more grief than pain."[6] This is no mere human love; this can only be agape love. He loves every one of them "with the affection of Christ Jesus."

I stand in awe of Paul's love for the Philippians. How do we, then, grow in having the affection of Christ for every single person to whom we are called to minister?

THE CURE FOR LOVELESSNESS IS FORGIVENESS

Sometimes people give gifts because they have a desire for us to change. Perhaps they see something wrong with us and want to help. For instance, if my twin brother sent me some anti-balding cream as a gift for Christmas,

6. Gordon D. Fee, *Paul's Letter to the Philippians*, New International Commentary on the New Testament (Grand Rapids: Eerdmans, 1995), 95.

I'd get the hint that it is now beyond obvious that I am going bald. If my parents sent me some tickets to a marriage conference called "Fixing Your Marriage before It Explodes," I might begin to think my marriage needs some work. If one of my sisters sent me a gym membership, I might think that they've observed that I've gained a few pounds over the years. These gifts are a way of saying that something needs to change. However, anti-balding cream, seminar tickets, and gym memberships do not guarantee that I will change.

The gospel is the gift that both reveals our need for change and guarantees that change will come. When the Father sent the Son into the world, that very gift was also the diagnosis that our condition was so bad that the only cure would be the perfect life, cursed death, and glorious resurrection of the Son of God. We failed to love others and couldn't fix it ourselves. We didn't need good advice or techniques, but a new heart and a new life. As the gospel reveals the gift that God longs to give us, it also reveals our condition that can only be cured with that kind of gift.

The gospel is also the gift that guarantees change. Along with justification inevitably comes sanctification.[7] Our "new self" is being renewed in the image of our loving God and merciful Savior (Col. 3:10; Eph. 4:24). Jesus Christ, who is in himself the greatest definition and manifestation of love, indwells us by the Spirit, conforming us to his loving heart and character.

Phil Ryken rightly points out that the cure for lovelessness is for us to know how much we are loved and forgiven by God.[8] He points to the story of the Pharisee and the prostitute in Luke 7. The Pharisee loved so poorly because he needed to be forgiven minimally, viewing himself as a pretty stand-up guy. The prostitute, however, loved passionately and lavishly because she knew she had been forgiven much (Luke 7:47). Instead of placing our own names in 1 Corinthians 13, we can, for our encouragement, also place Jesus' name there. Jesus is patient and kind toward *you*. Jesus doesn't keep a record of *your* wrongs. Jesus didn't seek his own welfare, but sought *yours*, though it cost him his life. Ironically, by realizing how radically you've been forgiven for being so completely loveless, you'll actually begin to love those around you.[9] When we understand forgiveness first as God's love to

---

7. As Westminster Larger Catechism 77 says, justification and sanctification are "inseparably joined."

8. Phil Ryken, *Loving the Way Jesus Loves* (Wheaton: Crossway, 2012), 70–73.

9. Ibid., 72–73.

us, it empowers us to be characterized by that same kind of love to others. That's why it is often helpful to return repeatedly to when Jesus forgave you and gave you new life. We must stand in awe of the radical forgiveness he showed to sinners like us.

That's precisely how Paul did it. Let's take a look.

THE CONTINUAL MOTIVATION TO LOVE IS GOD'S LOVE

The apostle Paul was no Mr. Hatch. His heart was enflamed with love for others because he knew how much he was loved. Paul said that he lived by faith in the Son of God "who loved me and gave himself for me" (Gal. 2:20). In fact, when Paul writes of God's love for sinners, he heaps on adjectives to describe the enormity of God's love and mercy. God doesn't just give grace, but "glorious grace" (Eph. 1:6). He doesn't just give grace to sinners, but lavishes the riches of his grace on us, so that we can enjoy "the immeasurable riches of his grace in kindness toward us in Christ Jesus" (Eph. 1:7–8; 2:7). The Father doesn't just possess love for sinners, but "great love" (Eph. 2:4). I think Paul would agree with Eugene Peterson when he writes, "In matters of God's grace, hyperboles are understatements."[10] You can never fully express in human language the glory and vastness of God's inexpressible love for sinners. As my friend Joe Novenson often says, "Multiply the love that your family and friends have for you, then multiply it by infinity and stretch it to eternity, and you still only have a small glimpse of God's love for you in Christ."

Paul himself was the one who wrote that "God's love has been poured into our hearts through the Holy Spirit who has been given to us" (Rom. 5:5), and Paul's cup was continually running over into the lives of sinners like himself, no matter how difficult they might be. He longed for the incredibly messed up Corinthians to know his "abundant love" for them (2 Cor. 2:4). He saw himself as being like a loving father and mother to the Thessalonians (1 Thess. 2:7, 11).

God's incomprehensible love for Paul was his motivation and power. When Paul personally experienced the love of God for a sinner like him, it filled his heart deeply with affection, not only for God, but for fellow sinners whom God loved, no matter how messed up they might be or how miserable

10. Eugene Peterson, *Practice Resurrection: A Conversation on Growing Up in Christ* (Grand Rapids: Eerdmans, 2010), 63.

they could make life for him or others. God's love stirred Paul's affections for others, but the motivation it gave him didn't end with affection. As the apostle John would later go on to write, "Little children, let us not love in word or talk but in deed and in truth" (1 John 3:18). Loving affection should lead to significant action on behalf of others. Because God poured his love into Paul's heart, Paul would pour his life out in love for others (Phil. 2:17).

THE ACTIONS OF LOVE

One of the first things Paul mentions is that love is kind (1 Cor. 13:4). This kindness is not only the internal desire but the tangible action of generosity toward others, seeking to help them in beneficial ways. It can often be the case that someone else's kindness is exactly what melts our own hardness. Listen to Augustine as he prayerfully remembers his initial interactions with the renowned preacher and bishop, Ambrose:

> The "man of God" received me like a father and expressed pleasure at my coming with a kindness most fitting in a bishop. I began to like him, at first indeed not as a teacher of the truth, for I had absolutely no confidence in your Church, but as a human being who was kind to me.[11]

Just as Ambrose's kindness had a remarkable, lasting, and memorable effect on Augustine, so our love, expressed in kindness, can impact the lives of those we serve. Throughout the Scriptures, often the most impact comes when an act of kindness is shown directly after significant offense has been given by something that was said or done. This is especially seen in the gospel, for God not only forgives sinners, which would be kindness enough, but then reckons them as righteous in Christ, then adopts them into God's family, and then invites them to the family table for the gospel feast![12] He heaps kindness upon kindness on the undeserving and then asks us to do the same to others.

I'll never forget totaling my truck when I was 16. My dad had bought me an incredible truck, with all the gadgets and upgrades necessary to make sure it could go where most other vehicles couldn't. I loved that truck. And I rolled it over . . . and over . . . and over on a country road in Indiana. Miracu-

---

11. Augustine, *Confessions*, trans. Henry Chadwick (Oxford: Oxford University Press, 1992), 88.
12. A great Old Testament story that mirrors the kindness shown to sinners in the gospel is the story of David and Mephibosheth in 2 Samuel 9.

lously, nobody was hurt at all, including me. I remember sitting on the side of the road, expecting my dad to kill me when he saw what I had done to the truck he had so graciously bought me. I'll never forget seeing him run toward me, embrace me, and say through tears, "At least we're just replacing a truck and not a son. I love you." I went home and we had dinner. That immediate response of kindness has been a lifelong paradigm for me in my own ministry, and God used that moment to begin drawing my heart to himself as I began to understand my heavenly Father's love and kindness toward me.

This is why it is so important, especially when a relationship has been damaged for some reason or another, to be quick in responding with a kindness that might be displayed in praying for them, calling them to get together for a meal, or surprising them with an encouraging letter, e-mail, or phone call. When we know that Someone loves us, we can show others tangible expressions of kindness, just as Christ has done for us in the gospel.

Love also believes and hopes all things. There's a wonderful story that H. G. Moule shares about Charles Simeon when he went to visit another minister, Henry Venn, and his family. Simeon was known for having a somewhat abrasive personality, and that was exactly what they experienced that day. Venn's daughters complained about Simeon afterward, to which their father responded by asking them to walk with him outside to pick some peaches from the trees in the backyard. They said that the peaches were not ripe enough to pick yet. Their father replied, "Well, my dears, it is green now, and we must wait; but a little more sun, and a few more showers, and the peach will be ripe and sweet. So it is with Mr. Simeon."[13] Venn's love believed that God was not finished with Simeon yet, and that God would continue the lifelong process of humbling him and conforming him to Jesus. Venn's love remained hopeful that Simeon would eventually change to have a more gentle and kind demeanor. And he did.

Ministry leaders often see the best and the worst of others, and when they experience the worst, it is crucial to keep in mind that love believes and hopes all things. If Paul didn't give up on the messy churches and individuals to which he ministered, then we shouldn't either. We can remain hopeful that God's love will prove victorious. And it will.

Experiencing God's lavish love and expressing our faithful love to others are crucial for longevity in ministry. Are you cynical toward others,

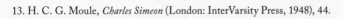

13. H. C. G. Moule, *Charles Simeon* (London: InterVarsity Press, 1948), 44.

or do you love them enough to believe that God isn't finished with them? Do you give up quickly when you experience disappointment or difficulty with someone else, or do you have love's hope that God will restore the relationship and renew their hearts? Love believes and hopes all things.

THE "SOMEBODY" WHO LOVES YOU IS JESUS

The neighborhood knew that something had happened to Mr. Hatch. They saw that his recent joy and enthusiasm was gone and that he was back to his old ways, so they decided to throw Mr. Hatch a big party with a large sign that said, "Everybody loves you, Mr. Hatch!" The story concludes: "Mr. Hatch dabbed at a tear with his handkerchief. 'I do believe'—he sniffed—'somebody loves me after all.' And then he smiled. And then he laughed. And then he hurried down to be with his friends."

One of the reasons leaders find it nearly impossible to love others at times is precisely because at those times they have forgotten the love of God for them. With this gift, the gift of the gospel, however, the mailman will never show up claiming to have had the wrong address. The gift will never be taken away because we've failed to earn it. It is ours forever. It is the gift of eternal love. And it isn't a generic message that says, "Somebody loves you." It is the specific and incredible message that the Father, Son, and Holy Spirit love you more than you'll ever be able to fully comprehend.

He loved you and gave himself for you.

Therefore, you ought to love one another.

Every. Single. One.

QUESTIONS FOR REFLECTION

1. In what specific ways has God shown you lavish forgiveness in the past and in the present?
2. In which aspect of love mentioned in 1 Corinthians 13 do you need to grow the most right now? Will you pray about this and ask another person to pray for you to grow in that way?
3. In what tangible ways did Paul love churches and individuals that either disappointed him or hurt him? How will this serve as a paradigm for you in moving forward in ministry?

8

DIVING INTO DIFFICULTY

THIRTY-ONE-YEAR-OLD logger David Gant and a friend, neither of whom had any caving experience, went spearfishing in an underwater cave at Lake Nickajack, just outside of Chattanooga, Tennessee, in order to catch the two-hundred-pound catfish of urban myth. Bypassing a clearly posted no trespassing sign, Gant and his friend jumped in. After only minutes of being in the water, silt was swirled up by their swimming and Gant panicked. With zero visibility, the inexperienced diver accidently swam deeper into Nickajack cave. Trying frantically to find a way out, he eventually found an air cavity thousands of feet inside the cave. It was there, drained of energy, that he clung to a stalactite, hoping that help would eventually come.

His friend made it out to call the local rescue squad. Enter "Buddy" Lane. Known as the "preeminent subterranean rescuer," and yet a quiet and humble man, he began planning the rescue, even while many thought it would just be a recovery (of a dead body). He spent significant time coordinating emergency services and communicating with law enforcement while personally preparing for the rescue. Only when all was ready did he head into the absolute blackness to find the lost caver.[1]

There are many pastors, including myself at times, who have concluded that ministering to others and serving in the church is a lost cause. Sometimes this conclusion is reached at the very beginning of ministry, but ordinarily it comes after trying countless times to rescue broken people, only to be beaten up, gossiped about, lied to, or just told to go away—repeatedly. In our minds, at times, it is really only a mission for recovery; rescuing someone or rescuing dying churches is a lost cause. Might as well just give up.

1. Hampton Sides, "Crawl Space," *Outside Magazine*, February 2002, http://www.outsideonline.com/outdoor-adventure/Crawl-Space.html

THE DARKNESS FROM WHICH WE DISTANCE OURSELVES

No pastor can describe sufficiently, though he has probably experienced painfully, the darkness that has enveloped the world and filled people's hearts ever since Adam and Eve made the dreadful choice of turning their backs on God and running in the opposite direction. Not only was their relationship with God torn to pieces and shattered, humanly speaking, beyond repair, but their relationship with others began to be torn apart and often characterized by tearing one another to shreds. The sad story of Scripture is situation after situation, relationship after relationship, where people "[lived] for themselves" (2 Cor. 5:15) and "did what was right in [their] own eyes" (Judg. 17:6) in an attempt to satisfy their selfish and insatiable desires. Fathers abandoned their children; husbands, and even kings, regularly cheated on their wives; women began to weave tangled lies to get what they wanted; children dishonored and even murdered their parents; dreadful and debilitating wars began between siblings, families, communities, and nations—and the list could go on *ad infinitum*.

But it gets worse. It gets darker. Even after God powerfully and decisively delivered his own people from Egypt, they didn't believe his word or trust his promises. They forgot his constant deliverances, and quickly and easily abandoned him in pursuit of bigger, brighter, and better things. All of them, like all of us, repeatedly walked over the very signs and words that God had mercifully placed all around them to warn them of the dangers of darkness. Yet, over and over God entered into the fray by calling, equipping, and empowering broken people with broken lives to be messengers of his breathtaking promises, which would never be broken, ever. But all of them were mocked, and many were killed. At one point, early on, God was so justly angry, furiously outraged, and rightly disappointed, that he told one of his servants to step aside so that he could destroy his rebellious, idolatrous, and foolish people and create a new and faithful nation (Ex. 32:10). They grumbled all the time and had even tried to kill him. Of course, their destruction would have been a great and unexpected gift to an exhausted and frustrated Moses!

Stop right here. Many pastors who've experienced the pain of ministry and incurred the wrath of others would love for that to happen. Let's be brutally honest here. In fact, it might be the greatest present, in their mind,

[handwritten margin note: always another chance — Moses]

that they could ever receive. For God to wipe out the very people who are making your life so miserable, so exhausting, and so stressful, and give you, in return, a congregation that always compliments and never criticizes your sermons, a congregation that urges you to spend time with your way-too-neglected family and spend as many hours as you need in private reading and prayer, a leadership core that makes sure you have a sufficient salary and regularly shares how God is working in their hearts through your ministry, and a thousand other blessings, would be the greatest joy you could ever experience. But God didn't do that for Moses then, and he won't do that with you now. Strangely, because God doesn't just destroy the difficult people we have to deal with, we find ourselves using phrases like "those people" to describe the ones we're called to love and serve, forgetting that the very same rebellion, selfishness, and darkness is in our own hearts.

When God doesn't destroy them, we're tempted to just remain distant from them. We stop entering into their lives, we stop praying for them, we stop weeping for them, we stop interacting with them. We don't dive in to rescue them. There are various reasons for this.

We Rehearse Hurts and Fail to Remember the Gospel

In Ephesians 2:11–13, Paul reiterates the importance of remembering the gospel. We all have to understand that we regularly have bouts of gospel amnesia. Our hearts and minds are gospel sieves that leak so fast that we have to frequently remind ourselves of the distance Jesus traveled to retrieve us from the "far country" (Luke 15:13). But when we fail to remember the gospel, we'll be quick to remember the hurt we've received from others. We'll remember the harsh criticism. We'll remember the sharp comment or dividing gossip. We'll remember all the ways that various people have either deeply hurt us or significantly disappointed us, and we'll be tempted to go far away from them—and remain there. If we rehearse the hurts and fail to remember the gospel, we'll never dive into the darkness.

We Fear Exposure

There is not a single human being on the planet who is omnicompetent, and yet most people fear being exposed as incompetent in some way. We avoid giving advice, because it might be written off as stupid. We try to counsel, but we know our counsel may be regarded as useless. We should evangelize, but then we might be asked a question we can't answer. You fill in the gap: where do you fear being exposed if you were to jump into the mess which the fall has created in every relationship, location, and situation that surrounds you every day? Fearing exposure keeps us from diving in.

We Don't Know What to Do

King Jehoshaphat acknowledged to everyone in Israel that he was clueless, and yet God used his ignorant trust to deliver them from a powerful army (2 Chron. 20). Why are we so afraid, most of the time, to admit that we don't know what to say, what to do, and in what direction to go? (I know that *I* don't want others to know that I don't know everything.) Being ignorant but trying to maintain a veneer of competence keeps us from diving in.

We're Cynical

Cynics are exceptionally wise when it comes to understanding the darkness, yet incredibly foolish when it comes to trusting the power of the gospel to overcome it. Things are simply so broken or too broken, and therefore nothing we could say or do would change anything at all. It's always been this way, and it always will be, so we might as well not even try. Cynicism will keep you from diving in.

We're Selfish

Selfishness is perhaps the simplest yet deepest reason. I like to read books, so I'd rather spend all day reading books. I like hanging out with nice people, so I'll avoid all the difficult ones and have a small group of people just like me. I don't want to get hurt, I don't want to engage, thanks for my paycheck, and I'll keep on doing what I want to do, even though it's not necessarily what needs to be done. I end up being more like a hired hand than a good shepherd (John 10:12). Selfishness will keep you from diving in.

Although, for one reason or another, we often distance ourselves from difficulty—whether relationally, emotionally, or perhaps even spatially (just stay in your office with the door closed and have your secretary tell callers that you're not available!)—Jesus took on our humanity and dove straight into our darkness, deep into our difficulty. Interestingly enough, while his unfaithful people and the rebellious world were becoming darker and darker, Jesus, the "preeminent rescuer," from all eternity and throughout history had planned and was implementing a rescue plan that would bring him closer and closer to us.

JESUS DOVE IN

Paul's confession: Christ Jesus came into the world to save sinners, of whom I am chief.

I find 1 Timothy 1:15 to be one of the most personally comforting—and, at the same time, most pastorally challenging—texts when it comes to understanding what we, as pastors, are called to rely on and embody before others. It presents to us a Savior who didn't turn his back on us when we (pastors included) had turned our back on him. It presents a Savior who passionately refused to distance himself from difficulty, but committed himself to becoming involved personally and intimately in our rescue. Let's take a quick look.

"*Christ Jesus came.*" Notice, pastor, that he didn't delegate the responsibility of jumping straight into the darkness. He didn't send angels. He didn't send tanks. He didn't send delegates. Christ Jesus came. Most of us don't like the responsibility of ministering to others when we know that it will be or might be heartbreaking, identity bruising, or soul crushing. If we do experience that, we may begin to daydream about doing something else. But Jesus didn't begin with avoidance ("Please, Father, I don't want to do this!"). He didn't begin with delegation ("Please, Father, *Moses* send someone else!"). He didn't begin with frustration ("Father, I will do this, but I really don't want to!"). He accepted the responsibility freely and with passion ("Behold, I have come to do your will, O God"—Heb. 10:7). Christ Jesus came.

"Christ Jesus came *into the world*." Not long ago, Francis Schaeffer characterized Western culture as predominantly concerned with personal peace and affluence. Who knew that the same critique could be leveled at the deep-seated idolatries sometimes lying in the deep recesses of a pastor's heart? As noted in a prior chapter, we really do expect people to act now like they'll only be able to act in heaven—perfectly. We really do expect the small portion of the world in which we live and minister to somehow escape the thorns, thistles, and constant disappointments and hurts of a terribly fallen world. We really do expect, and perhaps inwardly demand,

Stories/parables of soils

personal peace and affluence. When our expectations are crushed, we become disillusioned, disappointed, and discouraged—perhaps even angry and bitter—and stop entering redemptively into the lives of others.

When Christ came into the world, not everyone was waiting with banners flying and hearts eagerly waiting to receive him. "The world" that this text talks about was filled with relationships crumbling, hearts shattering, and people running away from him in such a way that when he got in their way or described the actual condition of their hearts, they (or should I say "we"?) began grumbling, accusing, and planning to silence him by crucifixion. You and I, pastors, were part of that world. We were part of the darkness that Jesus jumped into. Christ Jesus came into the world.

"Christ Jesus came into the world *to save sinners*." Despite what we may be tempted to think at times, he didn't come to save those who were exceptionally moral. Pharisees, outwardly moral though they may be, are inwardly sick. Jesus didn't come to save the upwardly mobile; the ladder of success can't get sinners high enough to get into God's presence. He didn't come to save the doctrinally faithful; doctrine may be straight, but the heart is still crooked. He didn't come to save the unusually sacrificial; give away all you have, and you still gain nothing. Nor was his concern national; Jews and Gentiles alike need redemption.

No. Any attempt to be good enough or to do enough good in order to gain God's favor falls short. Jesus came to save sinners. He came to save the bruised and broken, crippled and cast out, forgotten and forsaken, sinful and sorrowful. He came to seek and save the lost and the addicted, the angry and the hateful, the selfish and the unsatisfied. He came to save wives who hate and resent their husbands, and husbands who beat their wives and cheat on them. He came to save the annoying and the awful, the murderous and the rebellious. He came to save those who say hurtful words that pierce like a sword, who do things that deplete people's energy and damage others' souls. He really did come to save sinners and we, pastors, really are sinners.

"Christ Jesus came into the world to save sinners, *of whom I am the foremost*." Of all the darkness that Jesus jumped into, Paul saw his own heart as the darkest. Of all the sinners that Jesus came to save, Paul saw himself as the chief: "Put me up against perverts, killers, and whores, and I beat them all hands down. I was a mess, and I am a mess far greater than any of you."[2] Perhaps the greatest reason why pastors burn out inwardly and blow up outwardly at others is that we've forgotten that we really are the chief sinners within our churches or ministries. Surely, you think, it's that always angry person or the political manipulator or the betrayer or the liar or the gossip or the cheating husband or the porn-addicted teen or the constantly depressed person within your walls who is the chief sinner, but definitely not you. Interestingly, acknowledging his own deep depravity and need for grace was what enabled Paul to minister lovingly, patiently, and perseveringly to other major sinners—some of whom hurt him profoundly, personally, and often. But he never ran and he never gave up, because Jesus never gave up on him. The longer he was in ministry, the more passionately he called others "saints," but the more realistically he called himself "the least of the apostles," the "last of the brethren," and toward the end of his life "the chief of sinners." Christ Jesus came into the world to save sinners—even terrible, prideful, pastor-sinners.

Unbearable darkness, darker than we could ever imagine, both inside our hearts and outside in our world, is the bad news. The good news is that Jesus jumped in for you *and* for all those to whom you are called to minister.

THE CALL FOR US TO DIVE IN

I've been comforted a thousand times by Paul's urging of Timothy to stay in Ephesus (1 Tim. 1:3). In order to understand the importance of why Paul did this, we have to understand the external cultural climate and the internal church climate with which Timothy had to deal.

Wherever Timothy may have been staying, it's more than likely that as soon as he stepped outside he saw the temple of Artemis, one of the seven wonders of the ancient world. There an entire culture engaged in state-sanctioned idolatry and partook joyously and repeatedly in various forms of sexual immorality. When you look at how the culture initially responded to Paul and the gospel, you see an entire population racked by materialism, steeped in magic, and wholeheartedly committed to idolatry. But, by the grace of God and the work of the Holy Spirit, a church was born.

But even as Paul was leaving, he warned that the church would face incredible difficulty from within its own walls. Savage wolves within the

2. Dan Allender, *Leading with a Limp: Turning Your Struggles into Strengths* (Colorado Springs: Waterbrook Press, 2006), 55–56.

church, Paul said, would draw disciples away for themselves (Acts 20:29). And that's exactly what happened. Just read 1 and 2 Timothy. More than likely, some of the elders and leadership were mishandling Scripture and actively teaching things opposed to the gospel.[3] Men and women were being led astray while others were being extremely divisive. The church was becoming marked by immaturity, foolishness, and divisiveness. It takes only a quick reading to see how often Paul mentions the need for constant rebuke and correction (in love!) for those who were teaching error and living in ways that were not in accord with the gospel.

A hardened culture on the outside, thorough division on the inside—wouldn't you want to tuck tail and run? Common sense would demand that you run, and so might many people whom you might ask for wisdom to "get a sense of direction for where God is leading." Many think that Timothy was a timid man, and perhaps Paul knew that for any pastor, let alone a young one, these things may be too much to handle. Perhaps Paul knew that Timothy might have been making some phone calls to other churches or skyping with some search committees to see if God was calling him to another place, hopefully one that miraculously avoided the effects of the fall. Most of us joyfully and frequently skip from call to call, but more of us should heed Francis Schaeffer's advice and wait to be sufficiently "extruded" to another place.[4] Yet Paul was urging Timothy, as strongly as he could, to remain in Ephesus and finish the task he was called to do. He could urge him to do this because the same gospel that saved and transformed Paul (1 Tim. 1:15–16) would also save and transform the incredibly difficult and divisive people to whom Timothy was called to minister.

Read through the calls of Moses (Ex. 3) and Jeremiah (Jer. 1). Notice that both of them knew relatively well the difficulty that their callings entailed. They accepted their calls only after a time of responding weakly, cowardly, reluctantly, or even halfheartedly. I'd venture to say that the reason we, like them, hesitate to jump into the darkness is that we doubt

---

3. See Gordon Fee, *1 and 2 Timothy, Titus* (Grand Rapids: Baker Books, 1989), 40; see also R. Kent Hughes and Bryan Chapell, *1 & 2 Timothy and Titus: To Guard the Deposit* (Wheaton: Crossway, 2000), 26.

4. Francis A. Schaeffer, *No Little People*, in vol. 3 of *The Complete Works of Francis A. Schaeffer* (Wheaton: Crossway, 1982), 12: "The word extrude is important here. To be extruded is to be forced under pressure into a desired shape. Picture a huge press jamming soft metal at high pressure through a die, so that the metal comes out in a certain shape. This is the way of the Christian: he should choose the lesser place until God extrudes him into a position of more responsibility and authority."

the power of the gospel to change others and we really do love ourselves more than we love sinners who can hurt us.

In contrast, Jesus knew perfectly well that his mission of redemption entailed being rejected by his own people, constantly disappointed by his disciples, eventually abandoned by them, betrayed by one he loved, and crucified in excruciating physical pain while enduring the spiritual agony of his Father not only turning his face away, but also pouring out his unmitigated wrath on his soul. Even so, he accepted and accomplished his mission eagerly. Why? Because he passionately loves sinners like you and me.

The most common response to our fear of accepting God's call in Scripture is God's promise, "I will be with you." When you are called to jump *again* into the darkness of church politics, division, anger, disappointment, exhaustion, and confusion, you are not alone. God's presence and his grace will overcome your fear, ignorance, cynicism, selfishness, or laziness. The one who called you is the same one who dove in when you were dead and brought you to life. The one who called you is the same one who gave his life so that you might live. If we forget this, we may be tempted to run. But our commander in chief, the great Shepherd of the sheep, calls you not to retreat and urges you to dive back in, giving you the remarkable and heart-inspiring promise that, no matter what happens, he will be with you, his will will be done, and his kingdom will come—guaranteed.

DIVING IN WITH HIS STRENGTH

Sooner or later, if you make the choice to jump back in, you'll come to the end of your resources—and that is a good thing; perhaps you should even consider it a gift from a Savior who loves you. You'll actually feel weak and depend on his strength to make you sufficient; you'll actually feel foolish and ignorant, and you'll trust in his wisdom; you'll feel alone, and you'll trust in his promised presence, even if you don't sense that he's near. You may actually admit, like King Jehoshaphat, that you have no clue what to do, but you'll keep your eyes on your King (2 Chron. 20) and wait for his provision. Confidence in the power of God will lead to radical obedience to the call of God.

Jesus himself, the one who dove into your darkness and rescued you, and now calls you to dive in, is the one who promises his presence through the Spirit and his power through the gospel.

So what happened to David Gant? After thirteen hours of floating in absolute darkness, he was nearly out of oxygen from his air pocket. However, a mysterious wind blew through the cave, giving him the much-needed air to survive. Following behind this wind was Buddy Lane.

The reporter wrote:

[Gant] was dying—he was quite sure of it. The cave became a white tunnel. A pair of intensely bright lights approached. Everything was clear to Gant as he peered into the blinding luminance. "You're angels, aren't you," he said, "coming to take me away."

"Dude," Curry [another man on the rescue team] replied, "we've been called a lot of things, but never angels."

Buddy Lane's official report of the incident was quite simple: "Found victim alive. Everybody is happy."

Buddy Lane could've responded by saying that the mission was too difficult and that he might get hurt, and therefore that Gant should just have to reap what he sowed. But he didn't, and Gant is alive and well, even though he made a terrible decision that day. The story of the gospel is that Christ, our Rescuer, found us dead and gave us new life. He entered our darkness and brought us to the light. When thousands of years of planning the rescue came to a close, he took the plunge and suffered in our place.

Now he is calling you to enter that darkness in the lives of others, perhaps for the first time or perhaps for the thousandth time. Now he is calling you to bring the light of the life-giving gospel to those who are drowning in sin and, way too often, delighting in darkness. He is urging you to stay. He knows the pain and the exhaustion that you will definitely endure, but he will be with you, and he gives you the most powerful weapon on earth to accomplish the mission: the gospel of Jesus Christ crucified for sinners.

One day the entire rescue operation will be over, and all the difficulty and darkness will give way to the eternal happiness of the redeemed, who will see their Rescuer face-to-face forever.

God *will* use broken people to be instruments in his hands to rescue others from darkness. It's worth it. Jump right in.

QUESTIONS FOR REFLECTION

1. In what specific ways do you distance yourself from others, and what in your heart motivates you to do that?
2. How does the gospel mentioned by Paul in 1 Timothy 1:15 encourage you and give you a new motivation?
3. What specific situations right now require you to dive into darkness in order to be faithful to God's calling of you as a leader?

9

LONGING FOR A DEMOTION

IN THE YEAR 2000, author Rahna Rizzuto, a married mother of two, received a six-month fellowship to do research for a book in Japan. While doing the research, she came to the realization that she didn't want to be a mom anymore: "I realized I had lost myself a bit and I wanted to give myself more priority." When she arrived back home, she divorced her husband and left her children. Her book detailing her story of abandoning her family in order to make her own life the priority, *Hiroshima in the Morning*, was named a finalist for the prestigious National Book Critics Circle Award.

In a TV interview, she was asked a variety of questions, and one in particular got to the heart of the issue. Her response? Being a mother had made her do "that thing that I didn't want to do, which was *give up my life for someone else.*"[1]

I don't think the first response of anyone reading that story should be to point a finger and say, "What a terrible woman!" If we are reflective at all, we'll see ourselves in her—that deep down, at our core, we don't want to give up our life for someone else. Our hearts might say that being a Christian in general or a leader in particular has made us do what we really don't want to do, namely, give up our lives for someone else. This inborn, deep-seated selfishness is something that we are not only born with, but continue to struggle with, even after we've been redeemed.

How different is this story from the story of the gospel? This woman said, "I am a woman, and I will not give up my life for someone else." Jesus

---

1. Rahna Reiko Rizzuto, "'Hiroshima in the Morning': A Mother's Struggle for Identity," interview by Meredith Vieira, *The Today Show*, TODAY.com, March 2, 2011, http://today.msnbc.msn.com/id/41872847/ns/today-books (emphasis added).

says, "I am God, and I will serve others even to the point of death on a cross" (cf. Phil. 2:6–8). In the previous chapter, we looked at the fact that *we should jump back into ministry;* in this chapter we will look at *what our posture should be in ministry*—that of a servant.

AN ANALYSIS OF SELFISHNESS

Luther frequently commented that humans are *curvitas in se*—curved in on themselves. My visual horizon doesn't go much further than the end of my nose or the location of my belly button. My life is just that—*my* life. Whether or not I say it outwardly, I may inwardly admit that I am my highest priority. To give us a mirror to see this reality in our own hearts, the Gospels give us a ready-made illustration of this mind-set in none other than Jesus' closest companions, the disciples. In Mark 10, we get a glimpse of the personal and relational damage that is caused when we live life for ourselves.

Being Curved In Means You Focus on and Pursue Your Own Glory

The apostle Paul says to do nothing out of selfish ambition or vain conceit (Phil. 2:3), and yet this is exactly what the disciples were doing. Like we frequently do, the disciples defined greatness by self-glory, rather than by self-sacrifice. They wanted to sit in places of honor, where others would serve them and not vice versa. Like us, they treasured ascendency and promotion, moving to higher and higher places of honor, where others would respect and revere them more and more. This mind-set is not without its consequences.

This self-absorption made them and makes us blind personally. Notice that the disciples totally missed what Jesus said; they were blind to their Master's suffering. Jesus had just declared, "See, we are going up to Jerusalem, and the Son of Man will be delivered over to the chief priests and the scribes, and they will condemn him to death and deliver him over to the Gentiles. And they will mock him and spit on him, and flog him and kill him. And after three days he will rise" (Mark 10:33–34). At this point, anyone with an ounce of sympathy and compassion should have responded by comforting Jesus, asking more questions, learning more of what the kingdom is really like, and being filled with gratitude for the extent of Jesus' love for and patience with sinners. But this is precisely how they *didn't* respond. Focused on themselves, they became blind to the needs of others around them. How many times has the deep-seated sin of selfishness made us blind to opportunities to serve others faithfully?

This self-absorption also made them and makes us blind relationally. "And when the ten heard it, they began to be indignant at James and John" (v. 41). Their disease of "me-first-ism" was causing tremendous conflict within the group and damaging their unity.[2] And to most of these things they were absolutely clueless. It is usually the case that we are the last ones to know the damage we've caused and the conflict we've created. More often than not, we sincerely believe it has been caused by another person or a variety of external factors, and we rarely ask if we've contributed to the situation.

Being Curved In Means You Live by Your Own Strength

Jesus, knowing the baptism of wrath and justice and the cup of condemnation that he would have to drink, asked his disciples if they could drink the same cup and be baptized with the same baptism. "Of course!" they responded (see v. 39). Their selfishness caused them to underestimate the enormity of their own need and overestimate the reality of their strength. And all of this had an impact on everyone around them. Countless times the Spirit has been kind enough to point out that I was doing ministry in the flesh, in my own strength, and that by doing so I had become hardened. He still needs to point that out way too often! Have you overestimated your own ability?

Being Curved In Means You Seek the Easiest Path

The path that Jesus was on, as he had just told them, was a path that involved extreme humiliation, exhaustion, and suffering. This was the path of a servant. Yet the disciples wanted a quick appointment to places of high honor and prestige. They wanted to avoid the mundane, monotonous, difficult, and lowly work of serving others. Frequently, in ministry, if we can foresee that something may require diving deep into a situational mess, we try to avoid it somehow. If we foresee that something may require diving

2. On the concept of "me-first-ism" and how it influences ministry, see C. John Miller, *The Heart of a Servant Leader: Letters from Jack Miller*, ed. Barbara Miller Juliani (Phillipsburg, NJ: Presbyterian and Reformed, 2004), 307–16.

deep into a personal and relational mess, we try to avoid it somehow. There are a thousand ways to avoid the very work of servant ministry that we've been called to, and we often find one that will keep our hearts and heads above the fray and above the mess, so that those people or those situations won't hinder us from moving up whatever ladder we may be climbing.

Being Curved In Means Missing the Most Important Thing— the Gospel

One of the most incredible and sad results of our hardness and self-focus is that we miss clear opportunities to love Christ and cherish the gospel. The disciples missed an opportunity to repent when Jesus said, "You know that those who are considered rulers of the Gentiles lord it over them, and their great ones exercise authority over them. But it shall not be so among you" (Mark 10:42–43). If they had any sensitivity to the Spirit, any humility to respond, they would've said something similar to, "Jesus, you just nailed what is going on in our hearts. We want to be first, and lord it over others. Master, forgive us for what we've been motivated by, what we've said, and the conflict we've caused." But they didn't say that. They also missed an opportunity to rejoice. Jesus responded to them by saying, "Even the Son of Man came not to be served but to serve, and to give his life as a ransom for many" (Mark 10:45). I wish the verse continued with something like this: "And the disciples were amazed at Jesus' humility and grateful for his love, and therefore rejoiced together with great joy." But, again, it doesn't say that. Their hearts were self-focused and hardened, and sadly many of us can identify with their hardness. When was the last time you sincerely, genuinely, deeply loved Christ and cherished his work on your behalf?

At the end of this account, Jesus goes on to say that, as a servant, he will give his life as a ransom for many (10:45). This is the verse that gets at the heart of the matter for them and for us. The word *ransom* means a price paid to release someone from slavery or imprisonment. Jesus is saying that their greed and our greed are symptoms. He is saying that their pride and our pride are symptoms. He is saying that their conflict and our conflict are symptoms. The deeper cause is, as Luther said, our being curved in, enslaved to ourselves. These things are problems in my heart, and they are problems in your heart. These are the things that hinder us from valuing serving over being served. Is there a cure?

THE CURE FOR SELFISHNESS: THE SUFFERING SERVANT

In 1968, two researchers began a series of studies that came later to explain what would be called *the bystander effect*. Participants were placed in a room where various emergency situations were staged, such as smoke coming out of ventilators, someone falling down and hurting himself, or someone starting to convulse. What the researchers found was that individuals usually monitor the reactions of others to see if they should intervene. If others failed to step in to help, most of the participants didn't help. They called this *social influence*—we tend to only respond if others do. They also found that people would tend not to respond if they were given the erroneous information that somebody else would do so. They called this *the diffusion of responsibility*—just let someone else do it.[3]

That may be how *mere* humans in general respond, or how we in particular have responded to the needs of others around us, but praise God it is not the way Jesus, who became human, responded. Social influence and a sense of diffused responsibility, which so often impact our response, were absolutely antithetical to his response. We see this clearly and gloriously described in Philippians 2:6–8:

> [Christ Jesus], though he was in the form of God, did not count equality with God a thing to be grasped, but made himself nothing, taking the form of a servant, being born in the likeness of men. And being found in human form, he humbled himself by becoming obedient to the point of death, even death on a cross.

This incredible passage describes the breathtaking reality of Jesus' incarnation and humiliation. In the incarnation, "he became what he was not, but he ceased not to be what he was," and he took upon himself our flesh and donned a servant's towel.[4] In Jesus' humiliation on the cross, "the Life becomes dead and the Eternal Word is reduced to silence."[5] This should cause our hearts to stop and stand in grace-empowered and joy-filled awe at a God who is so contrary to what we think he would be like. He doesn't

3. Malcolm Gladwell, *The Tipping Point: How Little Things Can Make a Big Difference* (Boston: Back Bay Books, 2002), 28.

4. *The Works of John Owen* (Edinburgh: Banner of Truth Trust, 1991), 1:326.

5. Donald Macleod, *The Person of Christ* (Downers Grove, IL: InterVarsity Press, 1998), 215.

stand at a distance and remain indifferent, expecting us to serve him; rather, he humbles himself and becomes a servant. Even the Son of Man came, not to be served, but to serve (Mark 10:45). But was this merely an act of God's will as a reaction to what had happened? Or, perhaps, was it a purposeful revelation of the core character and heart of God?

I believe that the incarnation and humiliation of Christ reveal God to be, in his essence, a servant-God. Donald McLeod writes that "the impulse to serve lies at the very heart of deity. . . . It is his very form to forego his rights."[6] Paul, in this passage, declares that Jesus "made himself nothing" and took upon himself "the form of a servant." The life of a servant, or slave, revolves around the will and desires of his master. Jesus regularly and joyfully stated that he came to do the will of his Father, doing only what the Father said to do and saying only what the Father told him to say (Rom. 15:3; John 8:29; 5:30).[7] In fact, Jesus delighted in serving his Father so much that he called it his food (John 4:34). He came not only as the Son who fulfilled his Father's will, but as a Savior who served sinners. "Jesus, knowing that the Father had given all things into his hands, and that he had come from God and was going back to God, rose from supper," and washed his disciples' feet as a slave (John 13:3–5). Even in Jesus' day, the task of washing feet was considered by many to be so despicable that even some slaves were not expected to do it. But this was part of the process of becoming nothing.

Don't forget, being God himself made Jesus privy to all the perks, prerogatives, privileges, and rights of being God. For all eternity, Jesus was surrounded by a multitude of angels, singing his praises and standing in awe of his glory. Yet accepting the Father's will would entail being surrounded by cruel mockers and weak disciples. For all eternity, Jesus had delighted in the Father as the Father had delighted in him. Yet accepting the Father's will would entail not only being rejected by the Father, but also experiencing his unmitigated, unrestrained, full, ferocious, awful, and terrifying wrath. For all eternity, Jesus displayed spotless purity and unbounded holiness. Yet accepting the Father's will would entail being covered in our sin and suffer-

6. Ibid.

7. Murray J. Harris, *Slave of Christ: A New Testament Metaphor for Total Devotion to Christ* (Downers Grove, IL: IVP Academic, 2001), 96. See also Andreas Köstenberger, *The Missions of Jesus and the Disciples according to the Fourth Gospel: With Implications for the Fourth Gospel's Purpose and the Mission of the Contemporary Church* (Grand Rapids: Eerdmans, 1998), 108–11.

ing as "the greatest sinner that ever was," being cursed on our behalf.[8] So how did Jesus respond to the Father's will for him to become a slave, even to the point of death?

Like we may often do, he could have responded with *avoidance*. I'm sure he had quite a few things to do, such as upholding the universe by the word of his power and providing daily bread for millions. If anyone could have used the "I'm kinda busy so I can't do it" excuse, it was him. Like we may often do, he could have responded with *delegation*. Surely he could have found someone else to do the dirty work, someone else to do the more lowly things, while he remained primarily concerned with big things like creating galaxies, sovereignly controlling the flight of every bird, or telling massive storms where to send rain. If anyone could have used the "I'm too important for that line of work" excuse, it was him. Like we may often do, he could have responded with *frustration*. Eventually there comes a bending of the will to do the work, but the heart may not be in it. The task may be completed, but complaining will occur the entire time, guaranteed. Jesus didn't respond these ways. That bears repeating: Jesus didn't respond these ways. His heart never contemplated any excuse, but always and immediately responded passionately to the Father with, "Behold, I have come to do your will" (Heb. 10:7). He responded with the deepest act of humbling himself, *crucifixion*—suffering and dying the death we deserve, giving his life as a ransom for many (Mark 10:45).[9]

Throughout his life, especially and climactically on the cross at Golgotha, Jesus didn't just *act* like a servant; in the core of his character and fullness of his heart, he *was* a servant. Jesus showed us that to be God is to be a servant: "He did not exchange the nature or form of God for that of a slave; instead, he displayed the nature or form of God in the nature

---

8. See Martin Luther, *Galatians*, ed. Alister McGrath and J. I. Packer (Wheaton: Crossway, 1998), 152.

9. Notice MacLeod, *Person of Christ*, 220: "Never once does he in his own interest or in his own defense break beyond the parameters of humanity. He had no place to lay his head; but he never built himself a house. He was thirsty; but he provided for himself no drink. He was assaulted by all the powers of hell; but he did not call on his legions of angels. Even when he saw the full cost of kenosis, he asked for no rewriting of the script. He bore the sin in his human body, endured the sorrow in his human soul and redeemed the church with his human blood. The power which carried the world, stilled the tempest and raised the dead was never used to make his own conditions of service easier. Neither was the prestige he enjoyed in heaven exploited to relax the rules of engagement. Deploying no resources beyond those of his Spirit-filled humanness, he faced the foe and flesh and triumphed as man."

or form of a slave, thereby showing clearly not only what his character was like, but also what it meant to be God."[10]

Incredibly, even after the resurrection, Jesus performed the work of a servant by making breakfast for the failed disciples (John 21). Even at the wedding supper of the Lamb, Jesus will be our servant (Rev. 19:7). Worthy is the Lamb who was slain, to receive our unending and eternal gratitude and abounding praise!

LEADERSHIP: SET FREE TO BE ENSLAVED

Only the death of Christ, our suffering Servant-Savior, can set us free from our self-absorption that hinders us from sacrificially and genuinely serving others. It is the grace purchased for us by our Servant-Savior that shapes us into his image as servant-leaders.[11] In other words, grace not only frees us from slavery to ourselves, but also empowers us to enslave ourselves to others (Mark 10:43–44; Gal. 5:13). We have been set free by God's love to be enslaved to others in love.[12]

As noted above, there are many things that hinder this mind-set in us. We struggle to serve at all for numerous reasons, and even when we do serve, we can often do it in a very self-serving way![13] We may have entered into ministry with a love for people in general and realized that genuinely serving and loving particular people in particular ways would mean significant hardship, often thankless service, and mentally and spiritually exhausting ministry. But we have been bought with a price, and our lives are no longer our own! Grace doesn't just educate, and it doesn't just give an incredible experience. Grace equips and empowers us to serve. Serving those around us, even when it's exceptionally difficult over long periods of time, is exactly what we've been called to

---

10. Peter T. O'Brien, *The Epistle to the Philippians*, New International Commentary on the New Testament (Grand Rapids: Eerdmans, 1991), 216, 223–24. See also Hywel R. Jones, *Philippians* (Fearn, Ross-shire: Christian Focus Publications, 1993), 72; Gordon D. Fee, *Paul's Letter to the Philippians*, New International Commentary on the New Testament (Grand Rapids: Eerdmans, 1995), 208–10; D. A. Carson, *The Gospel according to John*, Pillar New Testament Commentary (Grand Rapids: Eerdmans, 1990), 463.

11. See Fee, *Philippians*, 210.

12. Harris, *Slave of Christ*, 80. See also Michael Card, *A Better Freedom: Finding Life as Slaves of Christ* (Downers Grove, IL: IVP Books, 2009), 69. This is also the central theme of Martin Luther's essay, "The Freedom of the Christian," in *Martin Luther: Selections from His Writings*, ed. John Dillenberger (New York: Anchor Publishing, 1958), 42–85.

13. Card, *A Better Freedom*, 57.

do. Thus, being a servant in a broken world to broken people in broken places entails having a gospel-centered heart, an others-centered mind-set, and difficult but incredibly rewarding labor.

Being a Servant Means Having a Gospel-Centered Heart

There is a reason why Paul emphatically says to do nothing from selfish ambition or vain conceit: he knows that this is our heart's natural default position. If we were honest, we'd admit that we want to advance at the expense of others, and that others should serve us and not vice versa. If we were honest, we'd admit that we want to be seen, acknowledged, and respected for being somehow superior to others (in our morality, abilities, accomplishments, etc.). This mind-set damages relationships and divides communities, as we saw with the disciples. The gospel, however, creates a default *gospel-centered* mind-set. Being a servant means taking our focus off ourselves and placing it securely on God's incredible grace, given in the gospel. The servant's heart first and foremost treasures the encouragement that we have in Christ, the comfort that we have from his love, and the participation in the Spirit that we enjoy (Phil. 2:1). This new default mode strengthens relationships and unites communities because it makes us others-centered. Is your heart gospel-centered?

Being a Servant Means Having an Others-Centered Mind-set

An others-centered mind-set begins with an internal condition and results in external action. The internal condition is humility: "In humility count others more significant than yourselves" (Phil. 2:3). The humility that Paul calls us to isn't a natural disposition of being quiet and reserved, nor is Paul intending us to understand it as low self-esteem (which, ironically, remains self-focused: "*I* am weak," "*I* stink," "*I* will never succeed," etc.). Humility is having a right estimation of ourselves as creatures and as sinners.[14] Also, as Tim Keller has wisely noted, humility is not just thinking less of ourselves but thinking of ourselves less.[15] The gospel creates an

14. See Jonathan Edwards, *Charity and Its Fruits* (Carlisle, PA: Banner of Truth Trust, 2000), sermon 6; see also Andrew Murray, *Humility* (London: James Nisbet and Co., 1896).

15. Tim Keller, *The Freedom of Self-Forgetfulness: The Path to True Christian Joy* (Chorley, UK: 10Publishing, 2012), 32.

internal condition of humility in our hearts that thinks less of "me" and more of "others." The needs of others, even if they have hurt or disappointed me, become more important than my wants. This gospel-humility, then, results in external action: looking out for the interests of others. Deep attention is paid, not only to our own needs, but primarily to the needs of others. Our heart's greatest desire and our life's great joy are in serving and providing for the needs of others, whatever those needs are and whoever the person may be. Is your heart others-focused?

Being a Servant Means Difficult Labor

Paul doesn't have rose-colored glasses on when it comes to serving. He's very clear that taking the posture of a servant will at times be exceptionally difficult and exhausting. He uses words like "struggle" and "toil," which imply laboring to the point of absolute exhaustion. He uses images like that of a farmer, soldier, gardener, slave, and others to show the long hours and hard work it will take.[16] I know in my own heart that when I begin to feel the difficulties of ministry, it usually confirms a desire to do something other than ministry, something much easier. But for Paul, when he felt the difficulties of ministry, it confirmed his union with Christ and his following of the example of Christ. Paul longed to "share his sufferings, becoming like him in his death" (Phil. 3:10).[17] Just as Jesus came closer as we ran farther away, and gave his life when we were dead in sin, the harsh realities of sin and brokenness and of conflict and division made Paul want to *serve more, not less*. The harsh realities and evidences of continuing need for grace in their lives made Paul more committed to ministry and service to others, not less. Service that costs nothing rarely accomplishes anything, but costly service embodies the heart of Christ and advances the cause of Christ.[18] Are you running from difficult labor or toward it? Does difficulty make you more or less committed to the cause of Christ and the bride of Christ?

---

16. Donald S. Whitney, *Spiritual Disciplines for the Christian Life* (Colorado Springs: NavPress, 1991), 126. See also David W. Bennett, *Metaphors of Ministry: Biblical Images for Leaders and Followers* (Eugene, OR: Wipf & Stock, 2004).

17. See Philip Graham Ryken, "Pastoral Ministry in Union with Christ," in *The Practical Calvinist: An Introduction to the Presbyterian and Reformed Heritage*, ed. Peter A. Lillback (Fearn, Ross-shire: Christian Focus Publishing, 2002).

18. Whitney, *Spiritual Disciplines*, 126.

Being a Servant Means Being like Christ

Leonard Bernstein, the late conductor of the New York Philharmonic, was once asked to name the most difficult instrument to play. Without hesitation he replied, "The second fiddle. I can get plenty of first violinists, but to find someone who can play the second fiddle with enthusiasm—that's a problem. And if we have no second fiddle, we have no harmony."[19] Playing second fiddle to others, with enthusiasm, is what leaders are called to do. By "putting on Christ" we are putting on the servant's towel and diving deeply, passionately, and sacrificially into the lives of those around us, just as he did. If you refuse, it won't be long until you hear the chords of disharmony in your relationship with Christ, your family, and those around you. If you humbly accept the role of a servant, there will be, over time, noticeable harmony, and at the end when you hear the music die down, you'll hear a voice telling you, "Well done, good and faithful servant. You have been faithful over a little; I will set you over much. Enter into the joy of your master" (Matt. 25:21).

QUESTIONS FOR REFLECTION

1. In what ways are you like the disciples in Mark 10, who desired to be first? Has it caused any friction among those who serve alongside you?
2. How would your internal thoughts and external actions change if the Spirit began to deeply form a gospel-drenched heart and an others-centered mind-set within you?
3. Whom is God calling you to humbly serve right now?

---

19. Quoted in Charles R. Swindoll, *Improving Your Serve: The Art of Unselfish Living* (Dallas: Word, 1981), 34.

10

FIGHTING—FOR UNITY

As GOD {Father, Son, Holy Spirit} model UNITY, they help us to do same!

I LOVE TO HIKE. For three years I was a rafting and mountaineering guide in the beautiful Collegiate Peak Range of Colorado. I often took clients and friends on hikes to some of this country's most beautiful and not-too-often-seen backcountry locations. One time I allowed a college student to lead the group up the trail toward the destination of White Peak. Minutes later he stopped and began running away as fast as he could and told everyone else, "Run!"

The frenzied pack of college students and their guides ran back down the trail and everyone was wondering what it was. A snake? A bear? Nope. A hornet's nest. When you hear the humming of the hornets, the only wise response is to run.

John Newton once told another young man that when "the old stale method of fire and sword do not work," Satan will surely seek to stir up fighting among the flock.[1] Not only Satan on the outside, but also sin inside people's hearts, makes the church a place where rumblings are frequently heard and felt: "An itch for disputing is the infection of the church."[2] I know this is why many *in* the church run away, and I fear that this is often why so many who get *near* the church end up running away as fast as they can. They can hear the buzz.

Yet the Lord in his sovereign purposes uses these trials to give church leaders experience and wisdom to navigate relational waters that they could not have received by mere books alone: "To learn navigation by the fireside will never make a man an expert mariner. He must do his business in great

---

1. *Wise Counsel: John Newton's Letters to John Ryland, Jr.*, ed. Grant Gordon (Carlisle, PA: Banner of Truth Trust, 2007), 94.
2. Ibid., 251, 258.

waters. And practice will bring him into many situations of which general theory could give him no conception."[3] To help navigate these waters and walk these trails, we will look at the gospel content, character, and competency necessary to fight for unity.

THE GOSPEL CONTENT NECESSARY TO FIGHT FOR UNITY

We are able to endure in gospel ministry when we keep the eyes of our heart squarely centered on him who is invisible (Heb. 11:27). If we are to endure actual or potential conflicts, we must fix our gaze on the Prince of Peace.

The Prince of Peace Has Made Peace with Us at Great Cost to Himself

Scripture is very clear that everyone has fallen short of God's glory, that there is no one who seeks after righteousness, that all the sheep have gone astray, and that the wages of sin is death, since God promises not to acquit the guilty. Our hearts were at enmity with God, and we were his enemies. He judged the entire earth in the flood, but he promised never to do that again.

Enter the Prince of Peace, Jesus Christ. He was wounded, crushed, chastised, and beaten, so that we could experience peace (Isa. 53:5–6). His body was torn and his blood was shed, so that those who were far off could be brought near (Eph. 2:14–17), and so that he could reconcile those who were alienated from the Father, hostile in their minds and at war in their hearts (Col. 1:20–22). He experienced the full curse and wrath of God (Gal. 3:13), so that we could be justified and have peace with God (Rom. 5:1).

God the Father was so committed to being at peace with us that he gave his only Son. The Son was so committed to being at peace with us that he fully and passionately gave his life. The Spirit was so committed to being at peace with us that he would effectually open our ears and hearts to hear the message of peace and experience that peace. God was committed to reconciliation, even at the great cost of his Son. Even after we have been redeemed, we wander and stray, yet the Lord seeks and gathers us back (Ezek. 34:16). Even after we have been redeemed, we grieve the Holy Spirit, but he never leaves us and perseveres in transforming us.

3. Ibid., 243.

intercede

The Prince of Peace Prays for Unity and Empowers Us for Unity

In John 17, Jesus reveals some of the deepest desires of his heart while praying to the Father—that our hearts would be rooted in a relationship with the Trinity and reflective of the intra-Trinitarian relationship of the Father, the Son, and the Holy Spirit, where they have loved one another perfectly, passionately, and purposefully from all eternity (see vv. 11, 20–23). He prays so passionately for this because this unity, amid all the differences within Christ's body (and there are many!), is humanly impossible.

It's humanly impossible for this kind of unity to be experienced among us because the differences that are actually part of God's sovereign creation become sources of significant conflict because of the reality of the fall. Different preferences and different ways of thinking, acting, speaking, and dressing all tend to create tension that occasionally erupts into minor discord or severe disruption (James 4:1–4). Yet God in his matchless grace doesn't leave us alone to strive in our own power to maintain the unity that the gospel has created (Eph. 4:3).

As Jesus moves toward the cross, he tells his followers that he will empower them for this kind of unity by his presence within us by the Spirit (John 17:23, 26) and his glory given to us (v. 22). Although humanly impossible, this kind of unity is achievable through the grace of God and the power of the Spirit, so that the body of Christ can be healthy and the mission can continue to move forward victoriously (v. 21). When you enter the next conflict, remember this truth and sense its power—the Prince of Peace prays for and empowers you and others for unity. *e.g 1 Cor 10 13 all temptation common to man, God faithful provide way 8]escape*

The Prince of Peace Has Proved Himself Trustworthy When He Calls Us to Enter the Storm

The gospel of the Prince of Peace puts everything we are called to enter into in gospel perspective. When we enter into the fray of large or small conflict, we enter as those who are gradually growing in understanding that these conflicts are sovereignly sent to us and specifically tailored for us, and we will be strengthened by the Prince of Peace himself as we seek to maintain the very peace he gave his life to provide. *How*

It must be settled in our hearts that we can trust the Prince of Peace as we realize that these conflicts are sovereignly sent to us. Ministry leaders, including myself, can often preach on, teach about, and counsel others

123

with the sovereignty of God, but when significant and severe conflict arises, we often flee in fear or attack in anger, failing to remember that a loving Father, a wise Savior, and an effective Spirit are working all things, even amid harsh words and hurt feelings, together for God (Rom. 8:28).[4] The theology that we often express in our responses to conflict often falls short of the theology we profess to know in our minds.

John Newton was counseling a young pastor with this very truth. Though we go through stormy conflicts, God "has the wind and weather at his command," and the "infallible Pilot" is at the helm.[5] Every leader's concerns "are in the hands of infinite wisdom and love, and of him who does all things well and nothing in vain."[6] "He has all hearts in his hands . . . (Ps. 65:7)."[7] Do you believe that God has sovereignly allowed and sent whatever conflict you may be in? Do you believe that he is doing whatever it may take to conform you and others to the image of Christ?[8]

We can also trust the Prince of Peace because these conflicts are specifically tailored for us. It's hard enough to believe that God has sovereignly sent difficulty to us for our good, but it goes even deeper, even more personal. Listen to how Ken Sande talks about it: "We will never suffer trials or be involved in disputes unless God allows them and is watching over them. In other words, every conflict that comes into our lives has somehow been ordained by God. Knowing that he has *personally tailored the events of our lives* and is looking out for us at every moment should dramatically affect the way we respond to conflict."[9]

God is more concerned with our conformity to Christ than with our comfort. We may, at times, be called to embrace conflict and hardship as "the chisel of God," but in his unfathomable love and infinite wisdom he will ordain it, allow it, and use it to conform us and the others involved more into the likeness of his Son.[10] How will knowing this "dramatically affect the way we respond to conflict"?

4. Ken Sande, *The Peacemaker: A Biblical Guide to Resolving Personal Conflict* (Grand Rapids: Baker Books, 2004), 22–29.

5. *Wise Counsel*, 93; see also p. 164.

6. Ibid., 181. See also p. 329.

7. Ibid., 220.

8. See also Bryan Chapell, *Holiness by Grace: Delighting in the Joy That Is Our Strength* (Wheaton: Crossway, 2001), 159–82.

9. Sande, *Peacemaker*, 62 (emphasis added).

10. Joni Eareckson Tada and Steven Estes, *When God Weeps: Why Our Sufferings Matter to the Almighty* (Grand Rapids: Zondervan, 1997), 114–25.

Finally, for our added encouragement, we can trust the Prince of Peace because these conflicts will come with the added grace of his strength given to us. God will always give us more than we can handle *without* him, but he will never give us more than we can handle *with* him. He promises to strengthen us (Isa. 41:10) and to make his power perfect in our weakness (2 Cor. 12:9). As we trust in the Prince of Peace, he will give us the power to pursue peace, even when it feels like the super-triathlon of conflicts.

To fight for unity, a leader must understand, with heart and mind, the reality that the Prince of Peace purchased peace for us at the cost of his own life, that he prays for us and empowers us to pursue peace with others, and that he has proved himself worthy of our trust as we wade through yet another conflict. He sovereignly sends and specifically tailors conflicts, and powerfully strengthens his leaders and his people as they walk through these harsh times to help bring us to maturity in Christ.

THE GOSPEL CHARACTER NECESSARY TO FIGHT FOR UNITY

Knowing the Prince of Peace personally and intimately is key to reflecting him faithfully through our character. Pastor Alfred Poirier writes, "In Christ we have a pastor whose hands are calloused by being about his Father's business—hands clasped in prayer, touching lepers, wiping eyes full of tears, and breaking bread. The first Pastor was a man of sorrows and familiar with suffering. The first Pastor was a lover of the real world even as he came to change the real world."[11] Yet Jesus came not just to teach us the skills of peacemaking, but to turn us into people who *are* peacemakers; not viewing reconciliation as a set of skills to be mastered, but viewing it as a "habit of being."[12] Therefore, it is crucial, when entering into ministry and enduring conflict in ministry, to remember that *what* we do and *how* we do it should flow first from *who* God is making us to be by his grace—peacemakers.

Leaders who reflect the Prince of Peace are *motivated by God's glory*. God calls us to love and adore his glory so that we can help others cherish and adore his glory along with us. However, it is possible for leaders or the

---

11. Alfred Poirier, *The Peacemaking Pastor: A Biblical Guide to Resolving Church Conflict* (Grand Rapids: Baker Books, 2006), 25.

12. Ibid., 13.

people in the pews to be motivated by vainglory (Phil. 2:3) or selfish desires (James 4:1–4). We are not called into any kind of ministry to pursue our own glory or to relate to others merely to fulfill our selfish desires; we are called into ministry so that we can spread a passion among our people and all peoples for the glory of God. It is often a good question for reflection to ask, "What am I being motivated by in the midst of this conflict?"[13]

Leaders who reflect the Prince of Peace are *humbled by their own sin*. By grasping the greatness of the gospel, a leader begins to understand the greatness of his sin. Only the blood of the Lamb, only the broken body of the substitutionary sacrifice, only the curse endured and death entered into by Jesus, can free the leader from sin. Only the work of the Holy Spirit can expose sin and empower the leader against it. Jack Miller urges young leaders to study the life of Brownlow North, who "self-consciously labored to speak from a heart knowledge that he was the chief of sinners."[14] Understanding the depth of our own sin and experiencing God's gentleness toward us will enable us to deal with others' sin in a spirit of gentleness because we come not as super saints but as fellow sinners. Are you more disappointed and grieved by your own sin than the sin of others? When conflict occurs, are you willing to listen to and potentially accept how others point out that you have contributed to the conflict?

Knowing our own sin and hating it the most, while taking refuge in the gospel of Christ, also makes leaders *gentle but courageous*. Paul says that we should seek to restore someone caught in sin "in a spirit of gentleness" (Gal. 6:1). Jesus was "gentle and lowly in heart" (Matt. 11:28), but was also able to wisely correct some and directly confront others. The Lamb slain is also the Lion of Judah (Rev. 4). Leaders are to reflect these character qualities of our Savior. Sadly, I can remember many times when my heart attitude and even my actions were harsh and vindictive, even as I was convinced, at the time, that I was being courageous. Leaders will often have to do or say some difficult things in a conflict, but there is a major difference between a drive-by shooting that leaves someone bleeding on the sidewalk and an EMT doing a tracheotomy so that someone can breathe. If I am gentle and courageous, my words and actions will be

13. This is the "Understanding Interests" portion of the "PAUSE" process outlined both by Ken Sande and by Alfred Poirier.

14. C. John Miller, *The Heart of a Servant Leader: Letters from Jack Miller*, ed. Barbara Miller Juliani (Phillipsburg, NJ: P&R Publishing, 2004), 69.

more like the EMT seeking to save a life than a gang member seeking to take someone out.

Knowing the sovereign Prince of Peace and the powerful Spirit of peace will enable leaders to remain *patient* with others. The gospel enables leaders to be more characterized by anguish than anger, by prayer for others than prideful gossip, and by patience than a quick temper. Leaders soaked in the gospel wait patiently for the most effective timing (Nathan approached David after nine months) to confront someone else. Leaders wait patiently and prayerfully for God to grant repentance to the others involved. Leaders don't angrily demand that a conflict go away, but patiently wait for the Lord to do his work in the midst of the chaos. The gospel leader understands that biblical patience isn't just waiting, but lovingly and graciously persevering amid frequent and sometimes severe provocation.

A leader can be patient because the Spirit helps the leader to be *perceptive*. This is clearly seen in the ministry of Paul, especially in his letters to the Corinthians and the Philippians. Though there are many difficult situations and chaotic conflicts to address, he begins by being *genuinely grateful* for the various ways he sees God at work in the lives of those he is addressing (see 1 Cor. 1 and Phil. 1). This is often how leaders do not respond in the middle of conflict—the difficulties become so large that they completely blind one to the reality that God is at work among the people. Newton, discussing people in his own church with whom he struggled, says that in most everyone there is "something to pity, and much to admire."[15] May God give gospel leaders the same perspective!

Gospel leaders reflect the Prince of Peace by *forgiving others* because they have been forgiven (Col. 3:13; Eph. 4:32). Jack Miller counsels others to "put on forgiveness as a lifestyle."[16] This forgiveness isn't just a feeling, it isn't forgetting what has happened, nor is it making excuses.[17] Rather, it entails absorbing the cost of someone else's offense against you and not exacting the penalty from them. It entails not dwelling on the incident,

---

15. *Wise Counsel*, 176.

16. Miller, *The Heart of a Servant Leader*, 197.

17. See Sande, *The Peacemaker*, 204–24; Poirier, *The Peacemaking Pastor*, 133–58; Miroslav Volf, *Free of Charge: Giving and Forgiving in a Culture Stripped of Grace* (Grand Rapids: Zondervan, 2005), 157–224; Dan Allender and Tremper Longman, *Bold Love* (Colorado Springs: NavPress, 1992), 13–20; Chris Brauns, *Unpacking Forgiveness: Biblical Answers for Complex Questions and Deep Wounds* (Wheaton: Crossway, 2010).

not bringing it up again in the future to use against someone, not talking to others about it, and not letting it hinder the relationship with the other person involved.[18] Luther has said that "the continual forgiveness of the neighbor [is] the primary and foremost duty of Christians, *second only* to faith and the reception of forgiveness."[19] We must learn early on that forgiveness will be a constant aspect of ministry, or else we will grow bitter, angry, and distant.

These are but a few of the character qualities called for that are engendered in us by the Spirit as we grow in Christ and reflect his image to others (for more, see 1 Cor. 13:4–7; Gal. 5:22–23; 1 Tim. 3:2–3). The content of the gospel shapes our character, which helps train us in gospel competency when it comes to fully engaging and remaining faithful in the midst of conflict.

THE GOSPEL COMPETENCY NECESSARY TO FIGHT FOR UNITY

God calls us, not only to *be* peacemakers, but also to be careful to *do* the difficult work of helping others pursue peace with one another. Developing the skills for peacemaking is something that takes great intentionality and considerable time, as it involves seeking wisdom, acquiring specific skills, and remaining faithful until there is resolution.

When I face conflict, I often feel totally incompetent to deal with it or else I selfishly desire not to experience discomfort or hurt, so I avoid entering into it. But sometimes I enter into a difficult situation too quickly, because I just want to get it over or think I know exactly what to do before taking the matter before the Lord.

A first step in addressing any conflict is to take the matter before the Lord in prayer and seek wisdom from him. Solomon asked for wisdom, and God gave it (1 Kings 3). King Jehoshaphat acknowledged that he didn't know what to do, but God gave him guidance (2 Chron. 20). God promises us that if we lack wisdom, he will give it abundantly and without reproach (James 1:5), and this peaceable wisdom from above will yield a harvest of righteousness (3:17–18).

God will often answer these prayers either by his Word or by leading you to others who are wise. Scripture is replete with wisdom on *when* to

18. Sande, *The Peacemaker*, 209.
19. *Luther's Works*, ed. Harold J. Grimm, vol. 21 (Philadelphia: Fortress Press, 1957), 149.

address someone, *how* to approach someone, and *why* it is necessary to do so at times. It's important that we search God's Word, so that we trust in the Lord and do not lean on our own understanding (Prov. 3:5). God may also answer your prayers for wisdom through the advice of other people.[20] I have found it priceless to have a few mentors who have been in ministry for decades and have an array of experiences to draw upon to guide me when I'm going through things I don't know how to handle. They will also be gentle in rebuking me if they feel I went about something in the wrong way! It's crucial to have others you can confide in with general aspects of a situation to receive guidance.

Another step in being faithful in the midst of conflict (personal or corporate) is to develop specific peacemaking skills. I do not have the space to develop in detail what these are, but every ministry leader should be personally equipped, and help to equip others, in conflict management by the thorough study of the materials put out by Peacemaker Ministries, led by Ken Sande.[21] These materials help to develop discernment as to when to deal with something and when to overlook it, and explain how to address an issue if it cannot be overlooked. They help to explore heart-level issues—how to get at the personal interests and potential idols that may be underneath the conflict.[22] It is also essential to learn how to wisely navigate the waters of correcting others in a way that will lead them into a better understanding of the situation and the gospel.[23]

Finally, I believe there are two often-overlooked issues when it comes to dealing with conflict: differentiation and reflection. Differentiation is "the ability to remain connected in relationship to significant people in our

---

20. It must be carefully kept in mind that I do not necessarily mean people within your own ministry. "Seeking wisdom" can sometimes be a cover for gossip ("Can you believe what this person is doing?!") or even the expression of self-pity ("Can you believe what I have to go through in ministry?!"). You must be wise and cautious in selecting whom you talk with and what details are necessary to share.

21. See especially the two books already mentioned by Ken Sande and Alfred Poirier. See also Paul David Tripp, *Instruments in the Redeemer's Hands: People in Need of Change Helping People in Need of Change* (Phillipsburg, NJ: P&R Publishing, 2002), 199–238; Tara Klena Barthel and David Edling, *Redeeming Church Conflicts: Turning Crisis into Compassion and Care* (Grand Rapids: Baker Books, 2012).

22. Their "PAUSE principle" is particularly helpful.

23. For instance, notice how often Paul uses the words *correct*, *rebuke*, *exhort*, and *admonish* in the Pastoral Epistles.

lives and yet not have our reactions and behavior determined by them."[24] This is difficult to do, as it is hard not to take the comments or actions of others personally and either avoid or attack them. Yet it is crucial if we are going to genuinely care for others in the midst of turmoil. Reflection is also necessary. After a discussion with someone involved in the conflict, or after the conflict has been resolved, it is necessary to take the time to prayerfully consider what was done well and what was done poorly, as well as what should be done differently next time the temperature begins to heat up. Wisdom often comes from experience, and experience often comes from mistakes, but we will not gain wisdom if we do not take the time to prayerfully reflect.

All of the above will enable a leader to remain faithful until the resolution of the conflict. The leader won't run away in fear or take a call somewhere else in the middle of a crisis within the body, but will stay committed to carrying through, prayerfully dependent on God and seeking to be faithful in helping believers love one another more and more.

FROM A HORNET'S NEST TO A BUBBLING BROOK

Let's go back on the trail for a much different situation than the one mentioned at the beginning of this chapter. In this situation, a group of men had hired another guide and me to get them to the top of a 14,000-foot peak. Let's just say that these men were not in the best shape and thought that it would be easy to go from sea level in Texas, fly to Colorado, climb a "14-er" in two days, and then go home and brag to their friends.[25] Sure.

Eventually they gassed out at about 11,000 feet and didn't want to go any farther. They were exhausted, defeated, saddened, and humiliated. On the way down, we got lost in a heavy fog that had rolled in. We sat for a while, waiting for the fog to lift, when the men became severely dehydrated. I sent the other guide to search for a stream, but he was gone too long for these Texans, so one of them decided to search on his own.

A few minutes later, we heard the man screaming. My heart flashed back to the hornet incident about a month prior. But this man wasn't

---

24. Bob Burns, Tasha D. Chapman, and Donald C. Guthrie, *Resilient Ministry: What Pastors Told Us about Surviving and Thriving* (Downers Grove, IL: IVP Books, 2013), 74.

25. Hikers often use the term "14-er" to refer to a mountain over 14,000 feet in elevation.

telling us to run away from something—he was loudly telling us to run toward something. He had heard trickling water, searched around for a while, and eventually found a stream. Needless to say, everyone followed and was refreshed.

That is why we must not run from conflict, but rather stay and fight for unity. If our hearts are motivated by the gospel and focused on the kingdom, we will not retreat when we hear the buzzing or experience the sting, but will stay as long as it takes and do whatever it takes, to see the Prince of Peace and the Holy Spirit transform a nest of hornets into a bubbling brook, where exhausted, defeated, saddened, and broken people can hear about, find, and experience the one who offers living water, Jesus Christ.

QUESTIONS FOR REFLECTION

1. Do you tend to respond to conflict by trying to avoid it or escape from it, or do you tend to respond by being too aggressive?
2. How does the gospel tell us we should walk through conflict? What specific texts can you look to for guidance, comfort, and strength?
3. Ken Sande says, "We will never suffer trials or be involved in disputes unless God allows them and is watching over them. In other words, every conflict that comes into our lives has somehow been ordained by God. Knowing that he has *personally tailored the events of our lives* and is looking out for us at every moment should dramatically affect the way we respond to conflict." How should knowing this affect how you respond in the midst of conflict?

11

IN IT FOR THE LONG HAUL

IN 1992, DEREK REDMOND finally had his chance, after almost a lifetime of training, to run the 400-meter dash in the Olympics. His heart was set on winning a medal, and his biggest fan, his father, was high up in the stands to watch it happen. But in the last 175 meters, Derek tore a hamstring. He pulled up immediately, began to hop, and fell to the track. Soon everyone saw Derek's father running down the stands as fast as he could. He leaped over the railing, ran past security guards, and ran onto the track. "That's my son out there," he yelled, "and I'm going to help him."[1] The love of this father for his son knew no bounds.

The steadfast love of the Lord endures forever. I want you to hear that again, because I need to hear it again: the steadfast love of the Lord endures forever. Even after that brief sentence, your heart should be bursting with worship and adoration of God. His mercies never come to an end, and they are new every morning, because God's faithfulness is great (Lam. 3:22–23). He will never, never, never give up on you (Heb. 13:5).

Endurance in ministry is rooted in seeing him who is invisible. As we behold his glory in Christ and hear the gospel of Christ, we behold a God who is full of steadfast love. If we do not see our heavenly Father and adore him for his steadfast love to sinners, then we will not show steadfast love to those we serve. The opposite is also true: as we behold the glory of God's steadfast love, we will be changed into that same image (2 Cor. 3:18).

1. Rick Weinberg, "94: Derek and Dad Finish Olympic 400 Together," ESPN.com, accessed March 13, 2012, http://espn.go.com/espn/espn25/story?page=moments/94.

BEHOLDING THE GLORY OF GOD'S STEADFAST LOVE: PSALM 136

When Luther said we have to beat the gospel into our heads, he wasn't being overly dramatic—he was being faithful to the Bible.[2] Psalm 136 hits our hearts and minds repeatedly with the refrain "for his steadfast love endures forever." As we survey this psalm to help lay a long-term foundation for faithful ministry, we'll see the power, patience, and perseverance of God's steadfast love.

Let's begin with the *power* of God's steadfast love. What is steadfast love? I've defined it as God's commitment to carry through on his promises, no matter what the cost. Out of sheer mercy and because of his love for sinners, he made a promise to those who would trust him that he would be their God and they would be his people. The Bridegroom took a vow to always be faithful to his bride, and this psalm celebrates that love and invites us to stand in awe of that kind of commitment.

The entire psalm invites us to think deeply and adoringly of God's "great wonders" (v. 4). His first move to help us do that is to point us to God's incomprehensible power and unfathomable wisdom displayed in creation (vv. 5–9). Have you seen the innumerable galaxies that the Hubble Space Telescope has revealed? Your God powerfully created all of those, and wisely governs and sustains them. Do you see all that the Lord accomplishes through the shining of the sun and the movement of the moon? This psalm says that this God is the God who promised to carry through, no matter what the cost.

Next we are comforted by the *patience* of God's steadfast love. Psalm 136:10–16 should shock us. Our powerful God has made a promise of commitment to people for whom the description "messed up" would be an understatement. The Bridegroom didn't choose his bride because she was lovely (see Deut. 7), but in order to make her lovely (Eph. 5:25–27). Yet notice that the power of God's steadfast love doesn't always remove difficulty. His people were in Egypt for four hundred years. They wandered in the wilderness for forty years! For the sake of brevity, let's just say that they grumbled and complained quite a bit, just as we do. Praise God that his faithfulness is not a response to our faithfulness or conditioned on it. Once he has made a commit-

---

2. Martin Luther, *St. Paul's Epistle to the Galatians* (Philadelphia: Smith, English & Co., 1860), 206.

ment to us, there is nothing we can do to invalidate his steadfast love or cause it to cease.

We see the patience of God's steadfast love as Psalm 136 details his incredible deliverance of Israel from Egypt and his leading of them through the desert. Why is God so worthy of worship? He never gives up on his people. He sent Moses to rescue them, and they didn't listen. Once they were rescued, they "turned aside quickly" (Ex. 32:8) and worshipped a false god. They were stiff-necked, rebellious, idolatrous, hard-hearted, and fearful—and God never gave up. Every boundary he set up they crossed over. Every word he spoke bounced off their hearts. Yet he never gave up. He was committed to carry through on his promise, no matter what the cost.

As great as the deliverance from Egypt was, it didn't change their foolish hearts. As faithful as God was to them in the desert, it didn't change their hard hearts. A greater deliverance was needed. A greater display of the steadfast love of the Lord was needed. But if God was righteous and holy, how could he remain mercifully and passionately faithful, despite their continual sin and idolatry that demanded punishment and wrath? His steadfast love is his commitment to carry through, no matter what the cost—and that cost would eventually be the life of his Son. With so much mercy, patience, and faithfulness displayed in God's beloved and precious Son hanging on a cross, crushed for our iniquity, how much more should we "give thanks to the Lord" because his steadfast love endures forever (Ps. 136:1, 2, 3, 26)? God's commitment isn't rooted just in his character, but also in his concrete action in the death and resurrection of Jesus Christ.

Finally, we can also cherish the *perseverance* of God's steadfast love in this psalm. There is nothing we can do to cause God's steadfast love for us to cease, and vv. 17–25 show that the perseverance of his steadfast love guarantees that there is nothing that others can do to cause his steadfast love to cease. There will be opposition to his plans and purposes, but God promises that he will rescue his people from Egypt and lead them to the Promised Land, despite any and all opposition, no matter how ferocious. It doesn't say that he *might* or that he *probably will*; it says that he *will*. Period. Nothing and no one can thwart his purposes. He is a God of steadfast love, and he will accomplish what he intends for his people. The power and patience of God's steadfast love guarantee that his love will also persevere through any and all external threats to his people.

Ultimately it was Jesus, the steadfast love of God made incarnate, who conquered any and all opposition to us receiving our inheritance (Gal. 3:13–14; Col. 1:13; 2:15). It was on the cross that God's ultimate care and love for us were displayed. It was on the cross that his ultimate commitment to us was portrayed. It was on the cross that his willingness to carry through on his promise was shown. It was the cross that secured steadfast love for the people of God for all eternity. Give thanks to the Lord, for his steadfast love endures forever!

ADORING GOD'S STEADFAST LOVE PERSONALLY

We should be overwhelmed as we think of God's steadfast love. Just think of the twelve disciples for a moment. They were constantly afraid, lacking faith, misunderstanding who Jesus was and what he said, forgetting, complaining, and arguing with each other about who would be the greatest. Frankly, we are just like them. Serious.

After a few of these incidents, I would be tempted to say, "Look, Father, I know I prayed and fasted all night and then chose these guys, but maybe I was wrong? Yep, I was definitely wrong. These guys are idiots and will do more damage than good. Bring me some new guys." But how did Jesus respond? He was constantly patient, loving, prayerful, enduring, and forgiving. He loved his own, even you and me, to the very end (John 13:1).

Please, I beg you, make this personal. How often did you harden your heart against God when you didn't know him? Yet he never gave up on you. How often have you wandered from him in your heart, even after you came to know Christ? Yet he never gave up on you. How often have you fallen short of his desires for you in your life, your family, and your ministry? Yet he has never given up on you. The good news is that he will never give up on you, because of his steadfast love, his covenant faithfulness, and his commitment to carry through, no matter what the cost. If you were lost, he came and found you. If you strayed, he gathered you back. If you were injured, he bound you up. If you were weak, he strengthened you (Ezek. 34:16).

The reality of God's steadfast love for you should have an enormous impact on your heart. It should make you genuinely humble, cause you to rest in his power and purposes, and cause you to hope in his future deliverance.

b.   The reality of God's steadfast love for you, ultimately displayed in the life, death, and resurrection of his Son, should make you humble. When I see from a distance or personally experience the disappointment of leading God's people, I am tempted to think that I don't struggle with what they struggle with. I am tempted to think that I am better. I am tempted to think that God is faithful to me because I have been so faithful to him. However, when I include myself with God's people and see, by the work of the Spirit, just how often my heart is in the same wrong place, I will be humble. I will be grateful for God's faithfulness to me, and I will begin to take my eyes and attention off myself and focus on God and on loving his people.

c.   The reality of God's steadfast love for you should make you rest in his power and purposes. When you are filled with anxiety and worry and fear in ministry, for whatever reasons, you must remember that your faithful God, full of steadfast love, is powerful beyond your imagination and wise beyond your comprehension. If his power hasn't kept something from happening to you, his wisdom must have a purpose for it and his love will strengthen you through it. We tend to forget this, and think either that God has given up on the church or that he has given up on us. In the midst of it all, we can be joyful and grateful that God is working in and among his people for his glory, even though we may not see it.

d.   Lastly, the reality of God's steadfast love for you should make you hope in his future deliverance. The hope of Scripture is a hope of certainty, not a hope of maybe. Maybe the weather will be nicer tomorrow. Maybe my team will be better next year. But the hope of grace is the hope of certainty. God *will* work in and among his people; that is certain, because his steadfast love endures forever. God will not allow any obstacle to keep his will from being done; that is certain, because his steadfast love endures forever. When we lose hope, we lose our strength to endure. When we are able, by the grace of God and the strength of the Spirit, to rejoice in hope, we joyfully endure as we expect God to be at work, both in ways that we can see and acknowledge, and also in ways that are invisible to us.

BEING CHANGED INTO THE SAME IMAGE AS WE BEHOLD GOD'S STEADFAST LOVE

God both *is* and *shows* steadfast love, covenant loyalty, to his people. The reality of the gospel is not only that the Spirit makes us new creatures

(2 Cor. 5:17), but also that the Spirit, gradually in sanctification, re-creates us into the image of the incarnate, steadfast love of God, Jesus Christ (Rom. 8:29). The more we humbly rely on and passionately cherish the steadfast love of God for us individually, the more we will reflect it toward those to whom we minister regularly.

During my first few years in ministry, my wife often heard a phrase from me that I look back on with grief. It was: "This makes me want to quit." It could have been an enormous, churchwide explosion of something, or it could have been something extremely small, like someone writing an e-mail or making a phone call that I thought could have been a little nicer. Externally, I tried to keep up the image that implicitly said, "I'm all in this. God is going to do great things. This is tough, but we'll get through it. God is faithful." Internally, though, I was saying, "I want to quit. I want to quit. I want to quit." At times, my only motivation not to vacate my post was that I was taught growing up, "Werners aren't quitters"—and I had never really quit anything hard in my life. Pull the bootstraps up. Grit your teeth. Keep on truckin'.

Needless to say, the distance between me and the end of my rope was a lot shorter than I thought. In his steadfast love, God began to point out areas in my life where I was unfaithful to him and hurtful to others. He began to point out areas where I pushed other people's buttons and disappointed them—and didn't even know it. He began to show areas where he was mightily at work, and I hadn't even seen it. He was everywhere doing so many great things, and I had missed out on the party. I hadn't depended on or delighted in his steadfast love for me, and I had forgotten about his steadfast love for his people—all of those precious, blood-bought saints whom he had given me the joy, privilege, and honor of serving in his name. He is still faithful to his process in my life and in yours of making us leaders who are in it for the long haul.

Let me offer a few tangible suggestions that will help our hearts remain full and overflowing, so that, by God's strength, we can remain in ministry for the long haul.

Meditate on Scripture and Rely on and Relish the Faithfulness of God to You

One of John Newton's favorite prayers for the young minister John Ryland was that the Lord would make his soul like a "well-watered garden":

"May you be like a tree in Jer. 17 growing in a stream of living water, your leaf always green and your fruit abundant, to the glory of the Lord, and to the benefit of all your connections."[3] A leader who endures is a leader who realizes his constant need to return to the source of living water—the Word of the Lord and the Lord of the Word (Ps. 1:2–3).

Meditate on Scripture and Rely on and Relish the Faithfulness of God to His People

The promise-making and promise-keeping God has made promises not only to you, but also to those to whom you minister. He will finish what he has started in their lives (Phil. 1:6). When you seek to minister to others, you are not alone. God himself is with you to help you, sustain you, and uphold you with his righteous right hand (Isa. 41:10). As you minister to them in a variety of ways, you'll find that God has already been faithfully at work in their lives. God will never leave or forsake you, and he will never leave or forsake them. This truth enables us to be leaders who endure for the long haul.

Develop a Heart of Joyful Gratitude for Where You See God Working

Part of the reason why I almost gave up was that I had become blind to what God was doing. When I was blind, I was unable to give thanks, and when I lost my gratitude, I also lost my joy. When I lost my joy, I lost my strength. When I lost my strength, I was on the verge of jumping ship. The Lord allowed my eyes to glance over an incredible and convicting statement:

> It would be unfair to suggest that the Church is unwilling to thank God for all His many mercies, but on the whole it is unwilling to indulge in detailed and specific thanks. If we were to train ourselves to recognize God's goodness act by act and detail by detail, many of us would come to think more highly both of God and of the Church. Much of our despondency comes from failing to see how much God really achieved.[4]

3. *Wise Counsel: John Newton's Letters to John Ryland, Jr.*, ed. Grant Gordon (Carlisle, PA: Banner of Truth Trust, 2007), 351.

4. H. L. Ellison, *Scripture Union Bible Study Books: Joshua–2 Samuel* (Grand Rapids: Eerdmans, 1966), 13.

If despondency can come from not giving thanks at all, or only doing it in general terms, then training ourselves to "recognize God's goodness act by act and detail by detail" can cause our hearts to overflow with gratitude and increase in joy. Then the joy of the Lord will be our strength (Neh. 8:10), and we will endure over the long haul with a heart overflowing with gratitude.

Develop a Heart of Expectance for God to Continue His Work among His People

I love how Paul tells Christians to rejoice "in hope" (Rom. 12:12). As noted above, we are to rejoice in what we have seen God do and in what we see him doing. Yet here Paul says that we are also to rejoice *in hope* for what God will do in our community and in the world.

Let me, however, give a necessary caution. In his book *Leading with a Limp*, Dan Allender shares the story of Jim Stockdale, who was the highest-ranking officer in the "Hanoi Hilton," the North Vietnamese prisoner-of-war camp. Stockdale shares why he survived and why other "optimists" didn't: "This is a very important lesson. You must never confuse faith that you will prevail in the end—which you can never afford to lose—with the discipline to confront the most brutal facts of your current reality, whatever they might be." He would say repeatedly to others, "We're not getting out by Christmas. Deal with it!"[5] The other soldiers would expect to be rescued by Easter. Easter would come and there would be no rescue. Then they'd say Thanksgiving. It would come and go. No rescue. Christmas then. Nope. Many gave up and died. The ones who endured were the ones who remained steadfast in their hope that they would get out, but they never set a deadline for it.

I did exactly what the "optimists" did. I put a date on when God was going to (or should) act. It would come, it would go, I'd be crushed, and then I would set the next date. "By this time next year, we won't be dealing with this anymore. It will be over," I'd say to myself. "By this time next year, we'll grow by this amount." I was setting myself up to be continually crushed. Only over time did I learn to have faith and hope that God and his purposes would "prevail in the end," and only over time did I learn to

5. Dan Allender, *Leading with a Limp: Turning Your Struggles into Strengths* (Colorado Springs: Waterbrook Press, 2006), 189.

not tell God when I expected him to act. He will act. His purposes will prevail. His timing is perfect. Rejoice in hope and endure for the long haul.

WE'LL FINISH TOGETHER

When Derek Redmond's father finally caught up to him on the track, he hugged his son and softly said, "I'm here, son. We'll finish together." Together, arm in arm, father and son, with 65,000 people cheering, clapping, and crying, they finished the race, just as they had vowed that they would.

The story of the gospel is different from Derek Redmond's experience. The heavenly Father loved his Son infinitely more than Jim Redmond loved his. Christ was in horrific agony, compared to Derek Redmond's hurt leg. The Father did not run toward his Son, but turned his back to him. Rather than declaring, "We'll finish together," the Father's silence meant, "You must finish alone!" Derek Redmond had 65,000 fans cheering him on, but Jesus was surrounded by hundreds who were mocking him.

Jim Redmond said, "I wasn't going to be stopped by anyone." But the Father stopped when his Son was covered in our sin. The Father could not but turn his back to such a horrific sight and pour out all his wrath on Jesus. That shows the Father's steadfast love for sinners like you and me. He loved his own—even to the end.

But the cross and the tomb were not the ultimate end. Once the price had been paid, the Father raised Christ from the grave. The race had been won.

That is God's commitment to pay the price in order to keep his promise. Because he did that to Jesus, when he now sees you or me or any of his people broken or fallen or about to give up, he runs out of the bleachers, carries us in his arms (Isa. 40:11), and says, "I'm here, son. We'll finish together" (Heb. 12:1–2).

> Our hope is in no other save in thee;
> Our faith is built upon thy promise free;
> O grant to us such stronger hope and sure
> That we can boldly conquer and endure.[6]

6. John Calvin, quoted in Ian M. Tait, "Calvin's Ministry of Encouragement," *Presbyterion* 11.1 (Spring 1985): 62.

QUESTIONS FOR REFLECTION

1. In what specific ways has God manifested his steadfast love and patience in your life?

2. If you were to spend a season asking the Spirit to show you where he was working in the midst of the people to whom you minister, what things might he show you? Could you respond by giving thanks "act by act and detail by detail"?

3. Who are the specific people or situations right now that are testing your endurance? How might the truths mentioned in this chapter guide you in responding to them?